THE
LEARNING
CONGREGATION

THE
LEARNING
CONGREGATION

A New Vision of Leadership

THOMAS R. HAWKINS

Westminster John Knox Press
Louisville, Kentucky

For information, address Westminster John Knox Press, 100
Witherspoon Street, Louisville, Kentucky 40202-1396.

Scripture quotations from the New Revised Standard Version
of the Bible are copyright © 1989 by the Division of Christian
Education of the National Council of the Churches of Christ
in the U.S.A. and are used by permission.

Book design by Jennifer K. Cox
Cover design by Kevin Darst

First edition
Published by Westminster John Knox Press
Louisville, Kentucky

This book is printed on acid-free paper that meets the
American National Standards Institute Z39.48 standard. ∞

PRINTED IN THE UNITED STATES OF AMERICA
98 99 00 01 02 03 04 05 06 — 10 9 8 7 6 5 4 3 2

Library of Congress Cataloging-in-Publication Data

Hawkins, Thomas R.
    The learning congregation / Thomas R. Hawkins. — 1st ed.
        p.   cm.
    Includes bibliographical references and index.
    ISBN 0-664-25699-6 (alk. paper)
    1. Pastoral theology.   2. Church renewal.   3. Organiza-
tional learning.   4. Christianity—Forecasting.   5. United
States—Church history—20th century.   I. Title.
BV4011.H345   1997
250—dc20   96-36564

To Jonathan,
who is a gift of God

Contents

Illustrations

Preface

The approach of the new millennium in 2001 is, in many ways, a statistical accident, an artificial milestone produced by how western societies calculate time. Nonetheless, the close of a thousand years of human history does have a remarkable ability to focus the mind, especially when it coincides with the loss of many taken-for-granted values and verities, institutions and inventions. We live during a time when congregations everywhere are buffeted by change and face immense challenges: HIV/AIDS, information technology and the Worldwide Web, a global economy, corporate downsizing, the aging of baby boomers, a continuing slide in financial support for congregations and denominations, and the growing marginalization of the Christian church in western society.

To propose that congregations face an adaptive challenge of immense proportions is an understatement. Many congregations are responding to this challenge with classic signs of work avoidance: holding onto past assumptions, blaming authority, scapegoating, living in denial, rushing to conclusions, or getting distracted by minor issues. Discovering a new vision of leadership may provide a way to break through these defensive routines and to mobilize churches for the adaptive work they need to do. At a recent conference on church development/redevelopment, a midlevel governing-body executive declared, "We once said that the three keys to success were location, location, and location. I've come to believe that they are leadership, leadership, and leadership."

I agree. The question is, *What do we mean by leadership?* The traditional heroic leadership that many people expect—and that many church leaders provide—is not the answer. Indeed, it may be part of the problem. But an alternative vision of leadership is possible: Leadership that mobilizes communities to address their adaptive challenges, that keeps attention focused on these challenges, that refuses to do people's adaptive work for them, and that creates a holding environment strong enough to contain their tensions and ambiguities. Such leadership involves problem finding or problem framing rather than problem solving. It consists not in providing answers but in mobilizing people to examine their assumptions about reality and to clarify their competing values.

Leadership's primary responsibility becomes helping people and communities learn the values, attitudes, and skills needed to minister at the speed of change. Leadership, learning, and ministry are thus deeply intertwined. To paraphrase the words of Henry Peter, Lord Brougham, spoken more than 150 years ago: Learning makes people easy to lead but difficult to drive, easy to govern but impossible to enslave.

This book is preliminary exploration of the relationships between adaptive work, learning, and leadership. It examines the nature of human learning as adaptation to change and what this means for congregations as learning communities. It then proposes a model for congregational leadership that attends to three distinct but interdependent dimensions of the learning process. Such leadership fosters individual learning among the congregation's membership. It facilitates team learning on church boards, councils, and committees. And it cultivates systemic or culture-based learning. These dimensions are bound together by a perspective that sees learning as comprehensive, relational, and public. This book provides both practical strategies as well as a theoretical framework for understanding the relationship between leadership, learning, and ministry.

These reflections emerge from my own struggle to reconcile my training as an educator with my leadership responsibilities in a variety of church organizations. I needed to draw together the various threads of seemingly contradictory tasks, responsibilities, commitments, and experiences into some larger, more encompassing vision. I am especially grateful to both the laypersons in the leadership development seminars that I have conducted and the doctor of ministry students with whom I have worked. They have all contributed in ways too varied and subtle to mention. My most profound insights into learning and ministry, however, have come in playful moments with my children, Robert and Jonathan.

I hope that my conclusions will enable others to make connections between—or at least to pose new questions about—responsibilities and commitments that sometimes seem irreconcilable and will assist congregations in undertaking the challenge of adaptive work.

Part 1

MINISTRY AND
THE SPEED OF CHANGE

1

Living at the Speed
of Change

We live in what some commentators call a permanent white-water society (Vaill 1989). We no longer experience the river of time as a slow, peaceful stream with quiet eddies and calm pools where we have ample opportunity to regain our equilibrium or to recoup our energies. We are instead white-water rafting through the rapids of social, technological, and demographic change. We are shooting down a foaming river filled with unexpected whirlpools and turbulent, rock-strewn channels.

Toffler (1991) describes the period from 1950 through 2025 as the "hinge of history." This period marks the end of the Iron Age, which began in the eighth century before Christ. In its place, a new "silicon age" is emerging. Information replaces steel girders and iron bolts. Computer chips are more important than assembly lines. New technologies quickly outstrip most people's knowledge.

And the speed of change is increasing. New information-based technologies erupt with breathtaking speed. Business cards once listed only a name, address, and telephone number. Now they are cluttered with incomprehensible chains of numbers and symbols: FAX numbers, beeper numbers, electronic mailbox addresses. It took twenty years to install one million telephones in American homes; it required only eighteen months to put one million cellular phones in American hands.

Technology is not the only factor fueling the speed of change. Shifting demographics also play a role. Since the Immigration

Act of 1965, new residents have transformed American society. The casual observer might conclude that DuPage County, Illinois, epitomizes the traditional white Protestant suburban community. Located immediately west of Chicago, it is a choice destination for families fleeing Chicago's urban problems. Appearances are deceiving, however. More than fifty religious communities, some very different from the traditional mix of Protestants, Catholics, and Jews, are supported by DuPage County's 700,000 residents (Marty 1993). Pakistani immigrants attend the local mosque. Sikhs and Hindus have their temples. East Asians participate in Buddhist temples and meditation centers.

This movement of peoples and cultures is a global phenomenon. Close to one-and-a-half million Japanese live in San Paulo, Brazil. One quarter of those living in Paris, France, are Algerian. Increasing numbers of young people leave the United States to seek employment in Eastern Europe, Asia, or Africa. New global telecommunications, computer, and transportation networks facilitate this movement of people and ideas, creating a dizzying cycle of transformation.

WORKING AT THE SPEED OF CHANGE

The speed of change is creating organizations that are flatter and less hierarchical. A new type of organization is emerging: the learning organization.

Creating the Learning Organization

Traditional organizations were hierarchical and stable. They were a pyramid—the most stable geometric and architectural form known to humankind—with lots of workers at the bottom and a few leaders at the top. Leaders could rely on their own knowledge because little information was needed to make decisions.

Today's explosion of information means that knowledge is now complex and widely dispersed. Rapid change forces people to seek continuous feedback about what is happening both inside and outside their organizations. Leaders can no longer rely on the small amount of information they alone can gather and remember. They need the insights, knowledge, and wisdom of others. This fuels a shift from hierarchical to participatory organizations. Vertical control is replaced by horizontal or reciprocal coordination in which workers are empowered to make decisions, solve problems, and self-monitor their own performance (Kanter, Stein, and Jick 1992).

Traditional organizations could be relatively simple because they had only a few, basic goals. Since change occurred slowly, the same task could be endlessly repeated. Organizations in today's white-water environment have to carry out multiple tasks in diverse settings. Organizations need to be fast and flexible.

These changes make learning a new organizational priority. Learning should not just help organizations adapt and survive. It should be generative. It should enhance the capacity to create. According to Senge, "This, then, is the basic meaning of a 'learning organization'—an organization that is continually expanding its capacity to create its future" (1990a, 14).

A learning organization is one in which individuals are always growing, learning, and creating. It is an environment in which there exists mutual respect and a willingness to examine both one's own assumptions and those of others. Learning organizations are characterized by an openness to experimentation and a recognition that failure is sometimes the price of risk.

According to Kim (1990), an organization's ability to learn dictates how quickly it can adapt to perpetually changing conditions. This same capacity for learning also determines how effectively an organization can initiate changes. Senge concludes that "the organizations that will truly excel in the future will be organizations that discover how to tap people's commitment and capacity to learn at all levels in an organization" (1990a, 4).

Biblical Faith and the Speed of Change

Biblical faith was born amid similar times of transition and transformation. Population migrations were reshaping the social and demographic maps of the ancient Near East. Empires rose and fell in their wake. Technologies we now take for granted, such as writing, were transforming how people experienced and organized their world.

Israel itself was a people on the move, made up of nomads, refugees, and a mixed band of peoples. As it wandered in the desert wilderness, Israel was betwixt and between. The old realities were gone, but the people were not clear as to the shape of the new world being born. They too lived on the hinge of history. Understanding that Israel's future depended on its capacity for taking risks and challenging inherited assumptions, Moses organized Israel into a learning community centered around the revelation of God's Torah.

Exodus draws a sharp contrast between the pyramids of Egypt and the new social organization of Israel. Pharaoh sits atop his pyramid of power. He seems to have total control. But he is so isolated that he can neither make good decisions nor adjust his behavior in light of changing conditions. As plague follows plague, the bankruptcy of vertical control becomes more and more obvious. Moses' Israel stands in sharp contrast to these pyramids of power. Israel is characterized by reciprocal coordination (Exodus 18), mutual respect (Ex. 20:1–17), and a commitment to growth, learning, and transformation (Deut. 6:4–9).

The early Christian church also emerged during a time of tremendous change and transformation. Roman roads and shipping routes snaked across Europe, North Africa, and the Near East, allowing for an unprecedented movement of goods, people, and ideas. In this turbulent environment, horizontal coordination rather than vertical control allowed the early church to expand rapidly. As Paul's letters suggest, the movement of couriers, evangelists, and missionaries could only have flourished in a context of mutual coordination rather than centralized control.

Boff observes that "the New Testament speaks of the charism of direction and governance. . . . [This] is the charism of coordinating the various functions—the various charisms—within the community. . . . Priests do not accumulate all functions for themselves. They integrate all services in a single unity" (1986, 94). Citing 1 Thessalonians 5:12, Romans 12:6–8, and 1 Timothy 5:17, Boff notes that the specific formality of this charism of governance and direction "does not reside in accumulation and absorption, but in integration and coordination" (28).

A New Model for the Church

North American congregations are heirs to this same heritage. Yet most congregations and church systems have operated in relatively stable environments where they accomplished a few simple tasks. The speed of change alters this situation, creating new ways of organizing for ministry and placing a new priority on learning.

Sharon Lempke's first pastoral assignment was in a congregation whose house of worship dated from the mid-nineteenth century. It consisted of a large sanctuary with pews and a small lecture hall. It architecturally symbolized the few simple tasks that this nineteenth-century congregation wanted to accomplish: worship and the transmission of Christian knowledge.

A few years later she served a congregation built in the 1980s. This congregation was housed in a sprawling building with multiple spaces for worship, education, service, and other activities. A myriad of programs occupied this building. It was staffed by a complex network of committees and volunteers engaged in a wide range of missional tasks. The building reflected how this congregation worked to accomplish multiple tasks in a highly complex, segmented environment.

The first sanctuary's pulpit was an ornate wooden tower that loomed over worshipers. It symbolized the pastor's hierarchical authority in a community where he or she was perhaps the only well-educated person. Preachers could command others based on their exclusive access to knowledge and skill.

These hierarchical, vertical structures were already disintegrating when architects designed the second church building. A small army of volunteers, many of whom were better educated and more skilled than the pastoral staff, carried out multiple programs in diverse, segmented environments. Monitoring the performance of these activities could not be centralized in the pastor. Coordination rather than control was required. Relationships were horizontally integrated rather than vertically controlled. Not surprisingly, the towering, ornate pulpit was replaced by a more modest lectern only a few inches higher than the pews.

Learning and Ministry

These changes demonstrate how new ways of organizing for ministry, prompted by the speed of change, make learning a new priority in church life. Consider the following vignettes:

We slip into the pew a few minutes before worship begins. As we leaf through the bulletin, we are impressed by the quality of the printing. Various type fonts have been used to produce something that is easy to read and pleasant to the eye. Noticing the church secretary sitting next to us, we lean over and express our appreciation. "Thanks," she says, "I resisted the office having a computer for a long time. I thought I'd never be able to learn how to use it. Now, after just a couple of months, I don't know what I'd do without it. And I've only learned a small part of its capacity."

The finance committee is discussing the disappointing results of the annual stewardship campaign. "We've been using the same method for five years," says the chairperson. "When we first started, our giving went way up. Although the response hasn't been that good the past couple of years, it has worked well enough. After all, 'If it ain't broke, don't fix it.' I just don't understand why people aren't responding this year."

It is Sunday morning after worship. A few of us are standing around in the fellowship hall, drinking coffee and munching doughnuts. We are informally discussing the pastor's relationship with the congregation, which is growing increasingly troubled and conflicted. One person says, "I have been a member here for thirty years. The same thing happens every six or seven years. It's the same conflict over and over. I even hear the same comments. The people involved come and go. But we keep repeating the same pattern."

Learning Through Ministry

All three vignettes reflect how a permanent white-water society is influencing congregational ministries—computers, deteriorating programs, conflict. They also highlight the importance of learning at the speed of change.

The church secretary discovered that learning a new skill—using a computer—was a change forced upon her. She resisted at first. She then gradually acquired new skills and knowledge, which enhanced her contribution to the congregation's ministry as well as her own self-esteem, confidence, and sense of personal efficacy.

The finance committee assumed that it could use the same strategy to underwrite the church budget year after year. Because it did not seek to improve its approach, no new learning and no adaptation occurred. Consequently, giving slowly decreased. The committee failed to realize that doing the same thing when conditions around you are changing is not really doing the same thing at all.

The congregation's history of conflict with its pastors showed that the whole system had not developed an increased capacity for new behaviors. Instead, it kept repeating the same pattern of miscommunication and conflict. It could not change its behavior because it had not preserved important learnings from previous pastoral conflicts. Without this capacity, it could not improve its partnership in ministry with a new pastor.

Learning at the Individual, Team, and Congregational Levels

These three vignettes illustrate another important concept. The need for learning is not limited to individuals. Learning occurs at three levels: the individual, team, and congregational levels.

The church secretary was an individual who initially resisted change. She then saw how the office computer could improve her personal performance as well as enhance the congregation's ministry. This prodded her to embark on a learning journey.

The finance committee adhered to the old rule, "If it ain't broke, don't fix it." Committee members saw no need to continually improve their performance. They did not sense the changes happening in their working environment. They did not learn from their own experience. Ministry teams—boards, councils, committees, and work groups—can fail to develop a capacity to learn. This failure diminishes their ability to change and improve continually the processes for which they are accountable.

The whole congregation had not learned from its past experiences with conflict. The congregational system repeatedly engaged in the same pattern of conflict with its pastors. If this congregation had learned from its past experiences, the whole system would have increased its capacity for a wider range of possible responses and behaviors.

Individual, team, and congregational learning mutually influence each other. Congregations that foster individual and team learning are more likely to find ways to capture and share new knowledge at the organizational level. A committee that does not value continuous learning is not likely to encourage individual learning. Truly effective congregations find ways to align individual, team, and organizational learning.

LEADING AT THE SPEED OF CHANGE

Organizations that work at the speed of change are characterized by a new type of leader. Organizations, according to Heifetz (1994), face two kinds of problems. Technical problems have clear-cut solutions that have been developed in the past. Organizations have a repertoire of technical solutions that they can apply to problems occurring under relatively stable conditions where past solutions still resolve present challenges. Adaptive problems, on the other hand, emerge because conditions have changed and the old technical solutions either no longer work or are counterproductive. Under such conditions, the organization must do adaptive work. It must develop a new response to the environmental challenge. "Leadership," Heifetz observes, "means engaging people to make progress on the adaptive problems they face. Because making progress on adaptive problems requires learning, the task of leadership consists of choreographing and directing learning processes" (187).

In an era of permanent white water, adaptive problems clearly outnumber technical ones. As a result, leadership becomes increasingly an educative task. Leaders are, above all else, educators. Senge describes leaders as teachers. Leaders are "responsible for building organizations where people continually expand their capabilities to understand complexity, clarify vision, and improve shared mental models—that is, they are responsible for learning" (1990a, 340).

Leaders are not responsible for teaching people the right or correct version of reality. They are responsible for cultivating learning environments where people transform their everyday experiences into new meanings that can guide their actions and shape their personhood.

Tomorrow's church requires leaders who are educators skilled in developing people and their gifts. The leader's basic work becomes shaping and reshaping meaning in a community where people engage together in the shared practice of ministry.

Church leaders traditionally gave attention to teaching Christians the proper doctrines and beliefs. In the emerging information era, they equip Christians with tools and strategies that allow them to learn continuously by reflecting on their everyday ministry experiences.

In the past, church leaders were recognized for their ability to grow churches. In the future, the ability to "grow" people becomes the key characteristic of effective and faithful leaders. The focus shifts from getting once-in-a-lifetime decisions for Christ to making lifelong disciples who continue to learn, grow, and serve.

When congregations become learning organizations, church leaders reframe their basic tasks and responsibilities. Pastors cease to perform ministry on the congregation's behalf. They instead foster learning environments where the whole people of God can shape and reshape meaning within a community of shared practice, continually clarifying those meanings in light of a deeper understanding of the revelation made known in Jesus Christ.

LEARNING AT THE SPEED OF CHANGE

Unfortunately, people's eyes usually glaze over when someone mentions learning. They immediately envision neat rows of school desks and the acquisition of irrelevant information. This is a far cry from the learning required in a permanent whitewater society. Learning in the future tense demands more than the passive consumption of information gathered by others.

The speed of change alters how we teach and learn. Mead (1978) describes two contrasting cultures: postfigurative and prefigurative. Each has a different perspective on teaching and learning. These perspectives are shaped by differing experiences of time and change.

Postfigurative cultures reproduce the past. Wisdom gleaned from past experience is considered a reliable guide for future generations because very few conditions change over time. "The essential characteristic of a postfigurative culture," according to Mead, "is the assumption, expressed by members of the older generation in their every act, that their way of life . . . is unchanging, eternally the same" (1978, 14). In a postfigurative society, elders teach children a limited number of eternal truths that have been preserved from past experience.

A prefigurative society reverses this relationship. Because the present is experienced as discontinuous with the past, new knowledge is continually constructed and reconstructed in order to cope with constant change. A prefigurative society invites all generations actively to reconstruct their knowledge, skills, and values. The younger generation always takes the lead in this process because it is more attuned to the emerging future.

Mead (1978) believes that the speed of change has caused the western world to shift from a postfigurative society to a prefigurative one. Anyone forced to ask their grandchildren to program the VCR has experienced this shift from a postfigurative to prefigurative world. This shift, according to Mead, forces us to reconsider how we teach and learn.

Traditional education was predicated on the slow, incremental change of a postfigurative culture. A few years of formal schooling could teach children everything they needed to know for a whole lifetime of work and family responsibility. The pressure of constant, turbulent change unravels this model of teaching and learning. Children growing up in a permanent whitewater society cannot master a lifetime's learning by attending school between the ages of six and eighteen.

Technological innovation stimulates the learning of new skills and knowledge. Political and demographic transformations spark the acquisition of new knowledge and values. The global map memorized in sixth-grade geography is relearned after the fall of the Soviet Union. The changing demography of North American cities means that long-term residents learn

Korean or Spanish, while new immigrants struggle to comprehend a culture very different from the one into which they were socialized as children.

Becoming a Society
of Lifelong Learners

Kegan (1994) argues that the modern world is changing so fast that we are all in over our heads. It is not just what the modern, prefigurative world demands that we learn—new behaviors to master, adaptive knowledge to learn, or emerging skills to acquire. It is also how we are expected to learn. Living in a permanent white-water society requires a new complexity of consciousness. The mental demands of modern life thus often exceed the capacity of our consciousness. We are in over our heads. Thus, Kegan continues, what we ask adults to do when they go back to school is "to go out of their minds" (1994, 272). Or better, to grow out of their minds, to develop a qualitatively different consciousness that can adapt to modernity's demands upon our mental life.

Pointing to these same trends, Knowles (1980) argues that schools must teach people how to be lifelong learners. If people know how to learn, they can constantly adapt their knowledge, skills, and values in a rapidly changing society. Learning replaces schooling in a permanent white-water society. Continuing education is the fastest growing sector in American education precisely because people are recognizing this need for lifelong learning (Apps 1988).

Schooling is the structured, formal way that society provides for learning. Schooling happens in classrooms with teachers. It has a specific content determined by someone other than the learner. It is usually limited to children and youth. Learning, on the other hand, happens continuously throughout the lifespan. It is a natural, human activity. Learning helps us to understand and give meaning to everyday experience. "Learning," writes Jarvis, "is the process of transforming . . . everyday experience into knowledge, skills, attitudes, and beliefs" (1992, 11). We learn as naturally as we breathe. Animals are born with instincts, people are not. We make our way through life by learning and not by instinct.

Learning, changing, and growing are thus interrelated

phenomena. "Learning is a response to change, but it also creates it," Jarvis observes. "Learning is a mechanism of adaptation, but it also has the capacity to evoke it; people learn to be safe; but learning is also a risk-taking activity" (1992, 210). Living at the speed of change challenges people to abandon the traditional postfigurative paradigm in which they are passive consumers of a schooling that reproduces what is already known. They instead become active participants in a prefigurative community of learners engaged in the construction and reconstruction of new knowledge, skills, and values.

Learning and Biblical Faith

Israel's psalms are full of a longing for learning that can transform the meanings that undergird human life. "Teach me your way, O LORD, and lead me on a level path," sings the psalmist (Ps. 27:11). Moses envisions Israel as a teaching and learning community that continually shapes and reshapes meaning in light of God's revelation. "Keep these words that I am commanding you today in your heart. Recite them to your children and talk about them when you are at home and when you are away, when you lie down and when you rise" (Deut. 6:6–7).

In his Farewell Discourse, Jesus constitutes his disciples as a new community of learning and teaching that will be guided by the Holy Spirit into a still deeper understanding of God's revelation made known in Jesus Christ. "I have said these things to you while I am still with you. But the Advocate, the Holy Spirit, whom the Father will send in my name, will teach you everything, and remind you of all that I have said to you" (John 14:25–26). A little later in the same Farewell Discourse, Jesus promises his disciples that "when the Spirit of truth comes, he will guide you into all the truth" (John 16:13). Jesus' words invite the disciples into a new community characterized by change, growth, learning, and transformation.

A focus on God's people as a learning community is not some recent trend or passing fad. It is neither a pragmatic response to a changing social context nor simply another version of the self-absorbed narcissism so prevalent in modern society. It is central to a discipleship that seeks to clarify and understand God's revelation, that seeks in all things to remain open to the transformation the Holy Spirit can work in personal and communal life. Learning is therefore an essential element in sanctification. "The goal of our teaching is the sanctification of persons and of congregations," writes Langford (1991, 65). Langford emphasizes that teaching "is for the sculpting of life" (65). Both learning and sanctification involve believers in an ongoing journey that examines the root assumptions controlling our lives and that constructs more accurate, apt, and fluid meanings to guide our lives.

A Revolution in How Churches Educate

Teaching and learning have always been part of the church's core mission. But teaching and learning happen differently in a permanent white-water society than they did in a stable, postfigurative world.

Children and youth are currently the primary participants in Christian education. According to one recent survey of mainline denominations (Roehlkepartain 1993), 60 percent of elementary children participate in religious education. Among adults, however, the percentage drops to 28 percent. Behind these statistics is the same postfigurative model that undergirds traditional public education: Everything necessary for a lifetime of Christian faith can be learned during childhood. Christian education is preparation for life, not something essential to an ongoing Christian existence.

Confirmation is sometimes treated as graduation from church education. Parents, youth, and congregations assume that a junior-high confirmand knows everything necessary for a lifetime of Christian faith. Once the *Westminster Confession* is memorized, for example, a young person has sufficient Christian knowledge for a lifetime of adult decisions and choices.

This perspective is inadequate for Christians in a permanent white-water society. Learning in the future tense must be continuous and lifelong. Martinson proposes that confirmation should not be a marathon during which all Christian knowledge is crammed into learners' heads. "Understood in the context of lifelong learning," he writes, "confirmation can afford to be less ambitious. It does not have to impart the whole counsel of God" (1988, 97). A similar analysis explains why so many youth ministries fail to attract young people. They are based on a postfigurative model in which leaders try to reproduce past or present Christian meanings in young people. "I suspect the stumbling block to full participation of youth in many religious traditions," Warren writes, "is that they are invited to participate in the reproduction of religious meaning but not in the true, original production of that meaning" (1994, 3). Successful youth ministries, on the other hand, involve young people in a dialogue with Christian tradition and their own contemporary experience. They become active participants who generate new Christian meanings through the construction and reconstruction of tradition and experience.

Christian education has frequently been teacher-centered. The key to effective Christian education was providing the right curriculum and recruiting the right teachers. The speed of change reverses this formula. Education in the information age is learner-focused. Multimedia learning, for example, allows users to make choices and to select pathways for their own learning. The learner, not the teacher, controls the pace and content.

Yesterday's Christian education was church based. Christian education took place in the Sunday school. Educational wings were divided into separate cubicles called classrooms. This physical arrangement mirrored a vision of education as segmented, fragmented, and functional. It assumed a split between the secular and the sacred. Christian learning took place in the classroom. It was then lived out or applied in the world.

Christian learning in a permanent white-water society is holistic. It happens in the home, the community, and the workplace as well as the church school or the sanctuary. Harris contrasts the new curriculum of education with the traditional curriculum of schooling. Education refers to "the interplay of the several forms through which education occurs . . . service, community, proclamation, worship, and teaching." Schooling, on the other hand, is limited to "a place called school, a form focused on processes of instruction, reading of texts, conceptual knowledge, and study" (1989, 64–65).

Learning at the speed of change occurs wherever and whenever ministry happens. It takes place across the lifespan, not just during childhood. It is not segmented into once-a-week classes. It pervades everything people do.

LEADING AND LEARNING:
PARTNERS IN THE DANCE OF CHANGE

Organizing for ministry, learning, and leading are not three separate processes. Learning and leading, according to Walker and Lambert, exercise a "dynamic influence on each other" (1995, 4). Leadership in a permanent white-water society is inextricably tied to helping people learn at the speed of change so that God's people can minister both faithfully and effectively in a time of turbulent social, demographic, and technological change. Ministering, learning, and leading are one interconnected dynamic. They are partners in a complex, ever-expanding dance of change.

Someone once described the church as a young person with white hair. The church has white hair because it is the bearer of the gospel's eternal message. Yet it remains forever young because it is always changing how its ministries proclaim God's love and embody Christ's service. Paradoxically, only by changing does the church remain the same. "Anyone who wants [the church] to live, as God's living congregation," writes Kung, "must want [the church] to change. Only by changing does [the church] remain what [it] is. Only by renewal is [it] preserved" (1968, 104).

Learning equips the church to remain the same while forever changing. Brueggemann observes that Israel's process of canon is a good model for contemporary teaching and learning. The canon, he writes, is "a process which partakes of stability and flexibility, continuity and discontinuity" (1982, 7). Religious learning always balances continuity with change, remembering with reconstructing, transmitting with transforming. This capacity allows the people of God continually to shape and to reshape the earthen vessels in which they carry the unchanging gospel of Jesus Christ.

Origen, a Christian teacher who lived in third-century Egypt, drew attention to the crucial connection between change, learning, and ministry (Williams, 1956, 47). After escaping from Egypt, Israel wandered forty years in the wilderness. During these years, God forbade the people to eat the previous day's manna. God instead required them to collect new manna each morning. What this really means, said Origen, is that teachers of the gospel should not set forth yesterday's stale doctrines for a new day. They should always bring forth new truth appropriate to the needs of each new day. Church leaders, according to Origen, are educators and teachers who foster environments where people discover afresh God's new manna of meaning through learning and ministry.

The next three chapters will look at these three components—learning, organizing for ministry, and leading. First, we will look at the nature of human learning and what it implies for congregations as learning communities. Next, we will explore how congregations can organize both for learning and for ministry. Finally, we will examine how leaders simultaneously foster ministry and learning.

1

Learning at the Speed of Change

A friend recently went white-water rafting in Idaho. Before her guide allowed her into the water, she had to memorize four rules. First, rest in the calm spots because there are always more rapids ahead. Second, when heading for a rock, lean into the rock rather than away from it. Third, never stop paddling. Fourth, let go of everything but your life jacket if you fall into the water. These rules also apply to ministry in a permanent white-water society.

Some people believe the river flowing from God's throne is always peaceful and calm. Change is a transitory blip on the screen. But my friend's guide has it right. Change is an inevitable, natural part of the river. There are always more rapids. Rather than lament the speed of change or resist it, we should go with its flow. After all, no one builds a hydroelectric plant on a peaceful stream. The rapids release the river's latent energy. This energy can power our ministries and fuel our discipleship.

We can best capture this energy by thinking counterintuitively. When heading for something that might harm us, our instinctive response is to swerve away. My friend's guide gave just the opposite advice: Lean into the rocks.

Our instinctive, habitual ways of doing ministry often no longer work. Traditionally, we developed a new program whenever we faced a ministry challenge. Membership is declining; organize an evangelism program. Giving is down; design a new stewardship program. But, as Mead observes, "we are not dealing with something that is responsive to a new program—even a very good program. We are engaged in a basic interaction between religious institutions and the nature of the social environment . . . we do not need a new set of programs. We need churches with a new consciousness of themselves and their task" (1994, 17).

We cannot manage our way out of the present crisis with better programs or more sophisticated marketing techniques. Developing a new consciousness of ourselves and our task requires generative learning. This, above all else, means thinking and acting counterintuitively. It means questioning how and why we do the things we do, continually re-inventing our ways of thinking and acting. In a permanent white-water society we can never stop learning just as my friend could never stop paddling. Learning in the future tense challenges us to think new thoughts and to test new behaviors.

Like my friend, we can let go of everything but our life jacket when the waves of change break over our boat and throw us into the foaming waters. That life jacket is the good news of Jesus Christ. Shortly after Paul evangelized Thessalonica, the Christians gathered there became anxious and worried. New ideas brought by other evangelists and teachers were troubling them. Unexpected events unsettled them. Meanwhile, the expected return of Christ had not happened. Paul therefore writes to reassure the Thessalonians, "because God chose you as the first fruits for salvation through sanctification by the Spirit and through belief in the truth. For this purpose he called you through our proclamation of the good news, so that you may obtain the glory of our Lord Jesus Christ. So then, brothers and sisters, stand firm and hold fast to the traditions that you were taught by us, either by word of mouth or by our letter" (2 Thess. 2:13b–15).

We ultimately preach a gospel of Jesus Christ, not a gospel of change. We stand firm by holding fast to scripture and tradition. Without this deep biblical memory, we cannot distinguish between what must be kept and what can be changed. Nor do we know on what basis to set standards or to make demands upon people. Our life jacket is the worship, prayer, and spiritual formation of God's people. Learning cannot be separated from discipleship.

LEARNING AND DISCIPLESHIP

The church as a community of disciples is, above all else, a learning community. The New Testament word for "disciple," *matheies*, shares the same Greek root as the word for "learning," *manthano*. Although *mathetes* occurs primarily in the Gospels and Acts, it connotes the important relationship between learning and discipleship among Jesus' followers (Rengsdorf 1985). Mark's Gospel, in particular, portrays Jesus as a teacher and his disciples as learners (Achtemeier 1975).

"We speak of the teaching authority of the church," writes Hull, "but seldom if ever of the learning authority of the church" (1991, 202). People and congregations lack the expectation that learning is central to what it means to be Christian disciples. Yet without learning, vital ministry cannot occur. Nor can vital learning happen without engagement in ministry. Mark Noll asserts that "to accept life in the world as a gift from God, to live as though a deeper understanding of existence leads to a deeper understanding of God requires dedicated and persistent thought, even as it requires dedicated and persistent spiritual vitality" (1994, 35).

Learning and Conversion

Stated theologically, learning involves conversion. Conversion means a shift from one basic perspective on the world to another. The New Testament word for "conversion" or "repentance" is *metanoia*. This word is a combination of *meta*, which means "through" or "above," and *nous*, which means "mind." Conversion is a change of mind. When we learn, we have a fundamental shift of mind. Learning involves a transformation in our perspective, a change in the mental maps through which we make sense of reality. And once we see the world differently, we cannot help but think and behave differently. As the mental maps that guide us change, the course of our lives also changes.

Genuine learning, like genuine conversion, is also a constant process rather than an occasional one. It is transformative, not incremental; lifelong, not a childhood phenomenon. Learning is not the same as acquiring more information. It means constantly recognizing, examining, and critiquing the fundamental perspectives through which we view life.

Paul tells the Romans, "Do not be conformed to this world but be transformed by the renewing of your minds, so that you may discern what is the will of God—what is good and acceptable and perfect" (Rom. 12:2). Too often we see the world not as God has created it but as we have been conditioned to see it by the cultural, social, economic, and political systems in which we are embedded. We see reality not as God sees it but as society wants us to see it. To learn is to question these assumptive frameworks into which we have been conditioned, to risk the transformation and renewal of our minds.

A little later in the same chapter, Paul suggests that the transformation of our minds involves us in counterintuitive behavior. Christians no longer act according to the expected values and virtues of their everyday world. Instead, he tells them, "Bless those who persecute you. . . . Do not repay anyone evil for evil, but take thought for what is noble in the sight of all. . . . Do not be overcome by evil, but overcome evil with good" (Rom. 12:14, 17, 21). How we see the world determines how we think and act. As we are converted to a new way of seeing, we act our way into new ways of being that may be very different from assumed ways of thinking and acting.

Learning and Revelation

If learning cannot be separated from conversion, neither can it be separated from revelation. Bernard Cooke (1990) has described three different ways that humankind can characterize revelation or divine presence. He describes the first mode of divine presence as special intervention. God is imagined as dwelling in a distant realm separate from human life. Revelation occurs through a special intervention into the human world, generally accomplished by some type of an intermediary. From this perspective, learning—as we are describing it—has no meaningful relationship to revelation. Revelation comes by special intervention and, at best, learning is little more than the rote memorization of an abstract, eternal truth.

Cooke's second mode of divine presence is participation in the divine. People regard themselves as sharing in the same essence as the Divine. Since we are made "in the image of God," we participate in the Divine. According to Cooke, this mode of divine presence has a tendency to focus on the spiritual realm since it is here that our resemblance to the Divine is imagined to be the strongest. Consequently, the natural and material world can be devalued. This perspective also downplays any linkage between learning and revelation. The hard work of learning is replaced by special insight and intuition.

Cooke describes the third mode of divine presence as a personal presence of the Divine that indwells within the material or natural world. Similarly, Barry (1992) argues that revelation is not something utterly foreign or alien to our experience. Otherwise we would not be able to recognize it. Instead God's revelation is always mediated through some human experience. "There is no experience of God that is not at the same time experience of something else" (Smith 1968, 35).

Cooke regards this third mode of divine presence as Jesus' most unique religious insight. Although revelation as a special intervention or as a participation in the Divine has often dominated Christian practice, everyday experience as the matrix of divine presence is central to any faithful interpretation of Christian life. According to Cooke, this third mode of divine presence characterized Jesus' Abba experience. "There is not a question of extraordinary occasions of God's word being addressed to him; rather it is the basic sequence of his daily human experiences interpreted by his Jewish religious understandings and lived with the focusing awareness of his Abba's presence to him that function as 'word'" (Cooke 1992, 64). Revelation is not something from the outside that breaks in upon us. Rather, for Jesus, "human experience is radically sacramental. Life's basic experiences possess a meaning capable of pointing to transcendence" (Cooke 1990, 365). The bridging medium of communication between God and humans "is human experience itself, the basic awareness of self and world existing" (363).

Such revelatory meanings, however, emerge not automatically but through critical reflection on everyday experience in light of other people's experiences and the community's experience as preserved in scripture and tradition. Cooke notes that "this raw word of daily experience requires interpretation—the entirety of education, formal and informal, is an effort to enable this interpretation" (1990, 363). What this implies is that "a Christian community must learn to hear itself, to become increasingly aware of the deeper meanings and dynamics of its own ongoing experience" (357). From this perspective, learning and revelation are two sides of the same coin.

But human experience can distort as well as reveal. Here too the link between revelation and learning becomes crucial. The Greek root that underlies the word "revelation" means "to uncover." As we engage in generative learning, we uncover the hidden assumptions behind our usual ways of thinking and discover how these have limited and even distorted our view of reality. We simultaneously uncover a fresh, unexpected vision of reality that discloses the world as God intends it to be. The challenge is to uncover, to reveal, the essential meaning of our experiences as revelatory encounters with the Holy.

The Gospels portray Jesus as harshly critical of religious hypocrisy (see, for example, Matthew 23). The Greek word *hypokrisis* comes from *hypokrinesthai* (a term from Greek theater meaning "to play a role") meaning "to play" or "to act." Religious hypocrisy is then a failure to be truthful about one's intentions before others, God, and even oneself. Jesus thus calls the church to live in truthfulness rather than hypocrisy (Kung 1968). To live in truthfulness is to strive continually to uncover the false assumptions into which we have been conditioned by our social world and which distort our ability to mirror the good news revealed in Jesus Christ. "To live in God's truth or reality," Kung writes, "demands truthfulness of a man [or a woman]. The realization of this truthfulness, however, depends upon the gift of God's grace" (40). Just as revelation and conversion come as unexpected gifts of grace, so does generative learning. It is not a human effort that succeeds because we try harder. It is instead a gift of God's grace in which we participate.

Anselm of Canterbury best captures this relationship between revelation, conversion, and generative learning in the first chapter of his *Proslogion* (1974, 92): "Teach us to seek You, and reveal Yourself to us as we seek; for unless You instruct us we cannot seek You, and unless You reveal Yourself we cannot find You. Let us seek You in desiring You; let us desire You in seeking You. Let us find You in loving You; let us love You in finding You."

Shaped for Ministry Through Ministry

The revelatory moments described by Anselm are encountered in everyday life as well as in a classroom. Classrooms are excellent for acquiring information. But daily experience is the best place to engage in generative learning. "Our focus," writes Little (1993), "should be adult learning within the context of ministry" (1993, 103). We are shaped *for* ministry *through* ministry. This interaction is at the very heart of learning at the speed of change. Ministry is that by which we are shaped as well as that for which we are shaped. People too often expect the church to nurture them through study so that they can then go out and apply what they have learned in the world. This is a false dichotomy. Ministry is not something we do after we learn what it means to be Christian. Learning occurs in, through, and under our ministry. Learning is not something we do in order to prepare for a life of ministry. Learning happens as we minister. Properly understood, discipleship encompasses both moments in the dynamic interaction between ministry and learning.

We speak of youth ministry in a holistic way that encompasses learning, ministry, and fellowship. But, Little (1993) complains, we split these apart when discussing adults. Congregations usually separate adult education from adult ministry. But are adults really that different from youth? Learning at the speed of change involves an interactive, fluid relationship between knowing and doing, acting and learning. As Moore asserts, "a reversal of expectations is needed so that congregations will see their caring and serving as central acts of Christian education, rather than as consequences of teaching certain attitudes and skills in formal educational settings" (1993, 35).

Harris observes that learning in the church "means taking those forms which ecclesial life presents to us [and] . . . lifting up and lifting out those forms through which we might refashion ourselves into a pastoral people" (1989, 41). Citing Durka and Smith (1976), Harris proposes that learning involves the development of more and more adequate mental models of reality. Learning equips people to form and to transform their mental models so that they are better able to shape and reshape their lives: "Educated persons are those whose lives—as complete entities from birth to death—are characterized by commitment to [mental] models capable of shaping those lives" (1989, 42).

Nurturing a Thinking, Learning Climate

Congregations sometimes treat people as a utilitarian resource. Church members' time and abilities exist to help the congregation grow, develop more impressive ministries, or offer a wider range of programs and services. Learning congregations invert this formula. The primary shift in a learning congregation is from using people to create a better congregation to using the congregation to nurture better people. Experiences in ministry become occasions for reflection and learning, for constructing a fresh vision of new life in Christ. These visions then guide new acts of ministry and service in Christ's name.

Church members, according to one recent study (Search Institute 1990), are hungry for such congregations. They want to be part of a Christian community where people discuss issues, raise questions, and learn more about themselves, their world, and their faith. Among adults, a *thinking climate* contributes more to the Search Institute's constructs of *faith maturity* and *denominational loyalty* than does the quality usually touted as a congregation's most important attribute—caring. There is, as Little concludes, "a genuine longing for some frame of reference and authority, some common history and language, some source of meaning, all of which point to a kind of expectancy people have when they think of the Bible" (1993, 101).

But what does it take to create and nurture this thinking, learning climate? What, after all, is learning?

WHAT IS LEARNING?

The need to understand our experience is perhaps humankind's most distinctive attribute. Animals are born with instincts. Human beings must learn. Tam, our family dog, instinctively knows how to be a dog. Our two sons, Robert and Jonathan, must learn to be little boys.

Tam is a dog; she does not learn to be a dog. Tam follows her instincts even when they no longer make sense. Before lying down, she will turn around in a circle several times. This instinctive behavior was purposive when wild cairn terriers lived in the Scottish highlands. A wild terrier turned round and round to flatten the grass over a spot where she was bedding down for a nap. Tam still repeats this instinctive behavior on our home's carpeted floor. She operates by instincts that do not respond to changed conditions. Although Tam can be trained, she does not truly learn.

Robert and Jonathan, on the other hand, live by learning. They must construe meaning from their experiences in order to know how to act. This ongoing organization and reorganization of experience captures the essence of learning. We give meaning to the experiences we have already had, or discover new meaning in our present experience, through this shaping and reshaping of our ongoing experience (Dewey 1933; Jarvis 1992). The fruit of this process—our construed meanings—guide our thinking, deciding, and acting.

Having spent many a sleepless night with our newborn sons, I am convinced that infants do not instinctively go to sleep. Babies must learn to fall asleep. Tam comes hardwired with a millennia-old bedtime ritual. Robert and Jonathan require repeated, predictable nighttime experiences before they learn to fall asleep. They transform these consistently and persistently reinforced experiences into patterns of meaning. These construed meanings then guide their bedtime behavior. None of this comes by instinct. It develops through learning.

Transforming Experience into Meaning

Learning begins when we ask why something happened as it did. We ask what it means. Our answer transforms raw experience into a deposit of remembered meaning (Jarvis 1992). As other experiences occur, they are connected to this remembered meaning. Built up over time, these frameworks of meaning distill into perspectives that shape our perceptions, guide our attention, and direct our actions (West, Farmer, and Wolff 1992).

Mezirow (1991) describes these frameworks as *meaning-perspectives*. Meaning-perspectives are the large, usually unconscious, frameworks into which our conceptual content is fitted. He contrasts meaning-perspectives to *meaning-schemes*, which are the actual content of our knowledge. Meaning-schemes are the specific beliefs, ideas, or concepts that are fitted into our meaning-perspectives.

Meaning-perspectives are the frames of reference provided by our culture, language, family of origin, and personal histories. They focus our perceptions, organize our concepts, and guide our actions. Meaning-perspectives are sometimes called "cognitive maps" (Sims and Lorenzi 1992), "mental models" (Weick and Bougon 1986), or "assumptive frameworks" (Bolman and Deal 1991). These meaning-perspectives play a critical role in how we think and act. Because events are complex and evidence is incomplete, people rely on mental models or assumptive frameworks to simplify the interpretation of events. Because these mental maps are unconscious, they are hidden from scrutiny. They nonetheless become the basis for our choices, decisions, and actions. This has some obvious advantages and some hidden disadvantages.

Advantages of
Meaning-Perspectives

In most situations, too much is happening for us to attend to all the information. Learning—transforming raw experience into remembered meaning—allows us to develop mental frameworks that group or chunk our experiences. These frameworks help us to cope with the flood of signals and stimuli coming at us. We use these mental frameworks to look for patterns of information. We pay attention to what fits our model and ignore everything else. This allows us to make sense of the flood of information that can potentially overload our senses. Without such frameworks, we could not make sense of the buzzing, blooming confusion of our experience (Gellatly 1986; Sims and Lorenzi 1992).

Relying on mental models is efficient. It saves us time, energy, and attention. It allows us to process vast amounts of information quickly. It simplifies the chaos of our experience and directs our perceptions. I need not pay attention to every cue and signal in a committee meeting. I recognize patterns and respond quickly to what is happening. Being freed from sorting through a mass of information, I have more mental energy to spend on the truly novel or the genuinely important.

Another illustration may help explain how mental models work. My father grew up in an era when farmers had few resources. So he saved all his used bolts, nuts, screws, and nails. In the tool shed attached to our barn, he had a shelf cluttered with peanut butter jars and coffee cans in which he stored his recycled fittings. When he disassembled old machinery, he carefully sorted each bolt and screw into a jar according to its size or length. He could then retrieve a half-inch metal screw or three-inch bolt when he needed it.

My father would throw leftover odds and ends into a large washbasin designated for whatever did not match one of his jars. To be cast into that washbasin was, for all practical purposes, to be discarded. My father could not bring himself to throw away anything that might potentially be useful. So he tossed it into the washbasin. But who had time to sort through all those random bolts, bent screws, wingnuts, rusty nails, and scraps of wire?

When he needed to repair a tractor engine, he quickly went to the jar that held the bolts he needed. He did not waste time sorting through a mass of unorganized fittings. The jars simplified his work. They allowed him to spend his energy on what was truly important rather than waste precious time and resources sifting through a disorganized mass.

Mental models are a lot like my father's jars and cans. We integrate new meanings into what we already know. We match something new with something already known. This conserves mental energy and frees our mind to concentrate on other tasks. An accountant was the church treasurer in one congregation where I served as pastor. His mental maps allowed him to glance quickly at financial statements and spot potential problems. The rest of us saw only numbers and columns. This ability was a real gift that helped the congregation anticipate and avoid financial difficulties.

A good pastoral counselor has similar abilities. As she listens to her clients, she almost unconsciously sorts through the words, phrases, and body language for patterns that match what she has come to know through her previous counseling experience or clinical training. Quick access to these mental models allows her to ask just the right question or to provide the right support. Knowing what to listen for, she can concentrate her energy and insight so that it produces the maximum benefit.

Disadvantages of
Meaning-Perspectives

Our mental models also have disadvantages. We can fill in the gaps incorrectly. I once served a congregation located in a rapidly growing community. Housing developments were sprouting in every field. New roads spread through woodlands with dizzying speed. Most church members were born into the church and had grown up in what was once a quiet, rural community. When asked about their community, they could not name these new roads or housing tracts. Even though they drove past them, they did not see these changes. Their mental map of the community was identical to the one that they had learned forty years before, when they were young adults. They could not acknowledge the changes happening around them.

Their inaccurate mental maps frustrated the congregation's attempts to reach out to new residents. These mental models caused church members to see a small, stable New England village intimately connected by family and history. Church members in that small New England community had mental maps that made it easier for them to navigate their community. Yet these same maps also meant that new possibilities for ministry went unseen.

Or consider Kathryn, a young woman who moves to a new city and begins attending a large, downtown church. The worshiping congregation is much older than she is. Kathryn signs the pew registration. She hangs around the narthex looking at the literature rack. She goes to the fellowship hour and stands near the coffee urn. Week after week she tries different strategies. Week after week no one speaks to her.

Kathryn's father and mother then visit for her birthday, worshiping with her on Sunday. Suddenly everyone speaks to her parents. They greet them in worship. They invite them to coffee hour. Kathryn remains invisible. But her parents fit the congregation's mental model of potential new members. The congregation's mental map focuses attention on people of a certain age and social class. The congregation's mental map saves time and energy, but it also means that Kathryn and others like her are overlooked.

Reliance on mental models means that we hear what we think someone said rather than what was really stated. We see what we think is there rather than what is actually before us. Mental models allow us to process lots of experiences quickly. In this way they help us. Their danger lies in allowing us to confuse what really exists with what we think ought to exist.

Our mental models also cause us to attend selectively to information. We look for what we expect to find, based on our preexisting mental models. Other cues are ignored. Meaning-perspectives direct our attention to some events. Meanwhile we overlook other equally important information. Someone starts to ask a question and we interrupt them with an answer before they have finished their sentence. Their opening remark drops into our mental category. We then cease listening to what they are actually saying and react to what our mental framework says they will say.

Finally, time and events may render our mental maps inaccurate. A trunk in my grandparent's attic contains some early twentieth-century roadmaps. They are very different from contemporary highways maps. Instead of blue, green, and red ribbons laced across the page, these maps give narrative instructions: "Drive down the road that leaves Springfield going past the Barre Hotel. There will be a large white farmhouse. At the next corner, turn left at the pig farm." Sometimes a blurry black-and-white photograph is interspersed with the text to ensure that travelers recognize the Barre Hotel or the corner with the pig farm.

Auto clubs designed these maps long before the current highway system existed. If I relied on one of these maps to travel from Springfield to Boston, I would quickly lose my way. Yet many individuals and congregations use mental maps just as antiquated as the ones in my grandparents' attic. We are reluctant to change these maps because we have invested so much time and energy in learning them.

Looking in the cockpit of a commercial airliner, the average passenger sees a dizzying array of buttons, lights, switches, and gauges. A commercial pilot has invested enormous time and energy in learning a mental map that converts all these dials and gauges into meaningful patterns. Precisely because the pilot has invested so much energy in building a mental map of these patterns, she resists abandoning the present cockpit design for another one.

It is the same with us. We invest a lot of time and energy in learning our meaning-perspectives. Therefore, we are reluctant to have them challenged. Reluctant, in fact, may be too mild a term. We cling to them fiercely. Because they become so deeply intertwined with our own identity, we develop defensive routines that prevent us from looking critically at our assumptive frameworks.

Kenosis and Learning

Our inability or unwillingness to examine the assumptive frameworks that justify our lives constitutes an essential part of our sinful condition. "The tragic condition of humanity," writes Scroggs, "is anxiously to create structures and security of existence precisely in the act of achievement" (1977, 16). We create structures of meaning and mental models of reality that prop up our own anxious self-identity. At least part of our sinfulness lies in our tendency to absolutize and then identify with these self-constructs. "Paul's proclamation," Scroggs continues, "is that salvation lies precisely in giving all of that project up" (16).

Jesus continually attacks his opponents as having eyes to see but not perceiving, as having ears to hear but not listening (Matt. 13:13). Their eyes have been conditioned to see what they expect to see; their ears, to hear what they expect to hear. Jesus challenges these socially and religiously conditioned assumptive frameworks. He invites his hearers to open themselves to a new vision of what God is doing among them. Even Jesus' disciples have difficulty recognizing him as the Messiah because their mental model of Israel's royal Messiah blinds them to the Suffering Servant who stands among them. God's self-revelation continually encompasses us, but we do not receive it because we refuse to question the very assumptions and mental maps that blind us to the divine self-disclosure.

Learning invites us to participate in Jesus' own self-emptying or *kenosis* so that we may open ourselves to God's gracious revelation.

> "Let the same mind be in you that was in Christ Jesus,
>   who, though he was in the form of God,
>   did not regard equality with God
>   as something to be exploited,
>   but emptied himself."
>
> (Phil. 2:5–7)

Only as we are willing to empty ourselves of our taken-for-granted assumptions and our cherished beliefs can we become open to receive the new creation God is already revealing everywhere around us.

A Zen tale tells of a young professor who visited a Zen master and asked to receive enlightenment. The master offered the young professor a cup of tea. The master poured the tea into an empty cup. He continued pouring even after the teacup was full. The tea spilled over the edge and filled the saucer. The master kept pouring. The tea ran out onto the table. The Zen master continued pouring.

As the tea began dribbling onto the floor, the young professor was no longer able to contain himself. "Stop!" he shouted. "It can't hold any more."

"Exactly like you," the Zen master replied. "How can you be open to receive enlightenment when you are already full of yourself?"

To learn is to be open to receive. In order to receive, we need to be willing to let go of cherished assumptions and beliefs. Learning requires that we be willing to question even those mental maps that secure our identity and establish our self-worth. Only then can we receive the revelation with which God graces us.

For too long we have thought about learning in terms of education. The root meaning of "education" is "to lead out." According to Plato, we already know the good, the true, and the beautiful. We have only temporarily forgotten these eternal realities. Education, according to Plato, reminds us of what we already know. Plato's definition has shaped the western world's understanding of education and of learning. But learning is ultimately not the same as education. A far richer understanding emerges when we link learning with revelation. Learning is something quite different from remembering what we once knew but have now forgotten. Learning requires us to experiment, to take risks, to challenge what we already know in order to embrace something entirely new that God may disclose to us.

The story of an artist marooned on a desert island illustrates this relationship between learning, risk, and revelation. The artist's most prized possession was a metal sculpture that he created over several years through painstaking effort and imagination.

As he molded and remolded his creation, he realized that he had grown as an artist and human being through his struggle with the metal. Although he was proud of his creation, he knew that he had grown beyond the very work that had challenged his talents and skills. So he went in search of more metal out of which to form another sculpture. This second sculpture would reflect even greater beauty and truth. To his disappointment, he found no more metal on the island. He could only produce another sculpture by melting down and remolding his first masterpiece. One can give two endings to this story. The artist may have decided not to face the pain of dismantling the creation in which he had invested so much creativity, imagination, and energy. Or he may have taken a painful last look at his sculpture and then lit the fire.

Resistance to learning is especially problematic in a permanent white-water society. When we are unwilling to examine or to alter our meaning-perspectives, we end up navigating the rapids of change with out-of-date, inaccurate mental maps.

We forget that our present mental models also developed through learning, through the transformation of raw experience into remembered meanings that now guide our perceiving, deciding, and acting. Just as our present mental models developed through learning, learning is how we question our assumptive frameworks and keep them flexible, accurate, and appropriate. "The focal concern of adult learning," asserts Mezirow, "especially in our culture with its high intensity of change, is with reordering one's life when dislocations occur and inherited recipes for problem solving do not seem to work" (1983, 1).

The Paradox of Learning

The paradox of learning is that just as learning socializes—and sometimes imprisons—us in particular meaning-perspectives, it also allows us to transcend and transform these inherited mental models (Jarvis 1992). Education, observes Bruner, is "not only a process that transmits culture but also one that provides alternative views of the world and strengthens the will to explore them" (1962, 117).

Three different outcomes are possible whenever we reflect

on remembered meanings in light of new experiences: (1) new experiences can transform the meanings accumulated in previous experiences; (2) they can adapt or alter these meanings without changing them substantially; or (3) they can simply add onto or reinforce existing meanings (Rumelhart and Norman, 1978).

Reflecting critically on a new experience can sometimes transform a meaning-perspective. Samuel grew up in a small rural community in upstate New York. His family always spoke negatively about New York City. It was dirty, dangerous, and crowded. Samuel's family frequently rehearsed stories in which New York City's residents were hostile and unfriendly.

On a visit to New York City, Samuel and his friends became lost while looking for the Museum of Natural History. A young Hispanic man noticed their dilemma, inquired whether they needed help, provided them with directions, and walked with them to the museum. This experience caused Samuel to reconstruct his prior meanings. A new experience transformed the meaning of Samuel's earlier experiences. This new meaning, in turn, changed Samuel's behavior toward New Yorkers in general and Hispanics in particular.

At other times, learning from a new experience means that we alter an existing meaning without substantially changing it. My son Robert understands that a dog is a four-legged creature, covered with fur, that barks. Most of his experiences are with Tam, a small cairn terrier. One summer we visited an aunt and uncle who have a Saint Bernard. At first, Robert thought his relatives had a pet bear. Later, he was able to integrate his different experiences, making connections between this new animal and his earlier construed meanings of "dog." His new experience altered the category of "dog" but did not substantially change it. He learned that dogs could be very large as well as very small.

In still other situations, critical reflection on a new experience simply adds to the meanings acquired through previous experience. This frequently happens in worship. Church members participate in the sacrament of the Lord's Supper. Each new experience of the Lord's Supper fits within the meanings construed from previous experiences of Holy Communion. We shape and reshape an experience, fitting it into the categories and qualities of already existing structures of meaning. In the process, these structures of meaning are intensified and reinforced.

FOSTERING A LEARNING CLIMATE

The critical reflection that transforms experience into meaning is not an automatic process, however. Another paradox of learning is that while we learn for the sake of action, we cease acting in order to learn (Jarvis 1992). We learn so that our mental maps of reality provide a better guide for our thinking, deciding, and acting. But to take a critical look at these maps, we must cease acting.

Creating Space
for Critical Self-Reflection

Vella describes this as a process of "doing—reflecting—deciding—changing—new doing" (1994, 12). She proposes some questions that we should ask when we are trying to slow down and reflect on the meaning of our experience:

1. What do I see happening here?
2. Why do I think it is happening?
3. When it happens, what problems does it cause?
4. What can I do about it?

These four questions are not unrelated to Holland's and Henriot's (1983) pastoral-hermeneutic circle. They propose a four-stage model: (1) insertion, (2) analysis, (3) theological reflection, and (4) pastoral planning.

The first movement, insertion, locates the lived experience of people and communities. These are the experiences that constitute the primary data for reflection. What are people feeling, seeing, hearing, experiencing? What is happening here?

The second movement is analysis. Analysis examines the causes behind the present experience, probes for consequences, identifies linkages to other experiences, and names relevant actors. It seeks to help participants grasp the historical and structural relationships at work in the situation. Through this analysis, people raise new questions about the assumptions they bring to the situation, about the mental models guiding their action. Why is this happening? What problems or challenges does it cause?

Holland's and Henriot's third movement is theological reflection. This entails an effort to understand this particular experience in light of scripture and church tradition. What light does the gospel bring to the situation? What new questions does it raise? What new insights does it suggest? What new responses does it open up? The final movement is pastoral planning, in which the individual or community discerns God's will as made known in their reflection, decides upon a course of action, and implements their plan.

Both Vella (1994) and Holland and Henriot (1983) are describing the same basic process of critical self-reflection. We stop acting long enough to question our assumptions, to explore our experiences with new eyes, to give them new meaning, and to test out these new meanings in renewed experience.

A group of teachers in a church-related school discovered that they had more and more nontraditional students in their classrooms. These students were older, had more life experience, and had been out of school for many years before returning to college. The teachers discovered that their mental maps for teaching did not work with these students.

The teachers engaged a consultant who helped them to examine their mental models and develop better maps and models for teaching this population. The consultant asked them to enroll in any adult education class where they would learn something they had never studied before. Reluctantly, the teachers agreed. After all, they had hoped the consultant would just give them some additional information about nontraditional learners. One took a gardening course. Another enrolled in a painting class. Still another attended an auto repair seminar.

The consultant asked them to keep a journal about their experiences in these classes. Once a week, the teachers gathered with the consultant to discuss what they liked or disliked about their classes. What did the instructor do to make them feel safe and welcome? To make them feel inadequate? What made learning exciting? What discouraged them?

As they shared from their journals, the consultant asked

them to develop a list of emerging principles for teaching non-traditional learners. This list was compared to how they already taught. The consultant also helped them to reflect theologically on the importance of their experiences and to ask what biblical themes spoke to their situation.

After about six months, these teachers shared the fruit of their learning with others in their church-related college. Their mental models for teaching had been made more flexible, appropriate, and capable of self-criticism. Through reflecting on their ministry experience, these teachers stopped acting long enough to learn for the sake of future action.

Whatever helps us to stop our automatic processing so that we can reflect critically on our experience will foster learning at the speed of change. Part 2 of this book will discuss a variety of strategies, tools, and techniques that can help individuals, teams, and congregations to reflect on their experiences and learn at the speed of change. These strategies, tools, and techniques make sense only when learning and ministry are seen as two interconnected movements of our Christian discipleship. Such an understanding of discipleship fundamentally alters how congregations organize for learning and ministry.

3

Portrait of the Learning Congregation

Learning at the speed of change may require congregations to slow down their thinking in order to reflect. Yet congregations are often characterized by compulsive busyness rather than by depth of meaning. As the pastor of an urban African-American congregation reported, "We believed that our spirituality should be guiding us. But we discovered that our programs were driving the ministry. So we stopped everything for two months and invited members to use their time to read scripture, pray, and reflect on what God was doing among us."

This is certainly one way to create space for reflective learning in a congregation. Yet how many of congregations would be willing to suspend all committee meetings and programmed events for two months? How do church leaders cultivate opportunities for people to reflect on their experiences and to deepen their understanding of scripture and tradition? In congregations where adult education is typically divorced from adult ministry, how do leaders foster environments where people are shaped for ministry by their experiences in ministry?

THREE CHARACTERISTICS OF LEARNING CONGREGATIONS

Cremin (1976, 1989) identifies three characteristics of education. These characteristics also describe congregations where depth of meaning replaces busyness in programs. Learning, Cremin proposes, is comprehensive, relational, and public.

Comprehensive

Learning is comprehensive because everything the church does offers an opportunity for people to name their experiences, to recognize their assumptive frameworks, and to make choices about what they know and how they know it. Teaching and learning are not limited to a single church subsystem called religious education. "The church does not *have* an educational program," writes Harris. "It *is* an educational program" (1989, 47).

Cooke (1990) observes that the early church was characterized by a mode of divine presence in which everyday experience was seen as sacramental and revelatory. In such a context, learning was comprehensive. Every experience could be a reflective opportunity in which the Holy might reveal itself. "God does not come and go in people's lives," Cooke notes. "Graces are not provided every now and then" (1990, 359). God instead stands at the door of everyday experience and knocks, hoping we will open the doors of perception and recognize God's ongoing presence and purpose in our lives.

Unfortunately, several historical trends undercut this comprehensive sense of revelatory experience. Christian worship gradually separated the sacred from the everyday. Certain times and spaces became holy, draining away the revelatory potential of ordinary life. Abstract ideas brought from the Greek philosophical tradition replaced people's experiences as a medium for understanding the divine. Official church structures and offices were borrowed from Rome's imperial government. These "official mediators" of God's power and truth (Cooke 1990, 56) served symbolically to distance people from God's presence and power. Christian life ceased to be a seamless whole where every experience is a matrix of divine presence. It is now separated into fragmented subsystems, arranged hierarchically and managed mechanistically. This context does little to foster learning that is comprehensive.

Machines Versus Organisms

Fostering learning that is comprehensive requires thinking that is organic rather than mechanistic. A machine is constructed. An organism grows; it is process-oriented. A machine only functions in a predetermined way. An organism changes, adapts, evolves. A machine is controlled from beyond itself. An organism is self-governing. Its structure evolves in response to feedback about its performance.

A machine is made up of many different parts that can be taken apart, handled separately, and then put back together. One can disassemble a car engine, spreading it across the garage floor, but it still remains a car engine. Living systems, on the other hand, have integrity. Understanding them requires seeing the whole, not the parts. If one takes apart a flower, one no longer has a flower. After the roots, stem, leaves, and petals are separated, they are never again a living plant.

When church leaders think mechanistically, DeGruchy (1986) complains, they treat the church as a machine made up of separate parts. Ministry is reduced to servicing the machine, keeping it properly functioning. Church leaders focus on manipulating the parts rather than on growing the whole. They become technicians who maintain programs rather than reflective leaders who equip a whole people of God.

Leaders who think organically, on the other hand, find opportunities for learning that is comprehensive and for ministry that is transformative. Learning and ministry are not inert objects (programs) or disconnected parts (a church school or an evening study group). They are comprehensive activities present in everything the church does. As Williamson and Allen (1991) assert, "Everything that happens in ministry and in the church offers people an opportunity to name the world. The question always to be asked is, In everything that we say and do, are we helping people to name the world in the terms of the gospel?" (105).

Linking Faith and Faithfulness

Learning congregations find multiple ways for their members to name the world in terms of the gospel—to link action and reflection, faith and faithfulness, thinking and doing. This happens in every committee meeting, every governing board session, every task force assigned to solve a problem. According to Brookfield (1986), "Learners and facilitators are involved in a continual process of activity, reflection upon activity, collaborative analysis of activity, new activity, further reflection and collaborative analysis and so on" (10). This rhythm of action and reflection, of knowing-in-action, characterizes congregations where learning is comprehensive.

Congregational life can occasionally separate action from reflection. Traditional Christian education sometimes encourages people to think about the Christian faith in one setting (a classroom) but to apply it in another (the home, a soup kitchen, a committee meeting). Committees and boards seldom see themselves as engaged in learning activities. They are action-oriented. They gather to *plan for* the church. They seldom expect to *be* the church as they plan, solve problems, or make decisions.

Yet these groups gather information, analyze data, and draw conclusions, all of which are the basic processes of adult learning. Learning happens whenever people stop automatically processing experience and ask themselves what is happening, why it is happening, and how they can respond more faithfully and effectively. Such moments are not limited to church school classes. They happen regularly in board meetings and committee discussions.

These moments of knowing-in-action are as important for adult learning as the time spent in a Sunday school class or a midweek Bible study. Church leaders, according to Little (1993), facilitate knowing-in-action when they train people in practical theological reflection. "This emphasis would mean that we learn not only to improve what we do, but equally important, that we be increasingly able to construct or formulate a body of knowledge that contributes to our theological frame of reference, undergirding all we do" (106).

When ministry and learning are interrelated, groups engage in faithful ministry and also learn about themselves and their faith. Reflection on ministry facilitates learning that is concrete, immediate, and continual. Such learning feeds forward into more faithful and effective congregational ministries. Learning thus fosters ministry even as ministry creates opportunities for learning. As people better understand their faith, they behave more faithfully. As they behave more faithfully, they act their way into a deeper understanding of Christian faith, which promotes a new depth in faithfulness.

Pastors and other church leaders play a crucial role in equipping people for practical theological reflection. They help church members to interpret the meaning of experience, Carroll proposes, by engaging them in a process of "framing or reframing [experience] in terms of the gospel and exploring responses to [experience] in ways that express Christian identity" (1991, 100).

Some Guidelines for
Knowing-in-Action

Knowing-in-action is as much an art as a science. There are no easy techniques or simple methods. Yet there are guidelines. Carroll (1991) provides two criteria for such reflection: background factors and foreground factors. His background factors include (1) participants' personal histories and stories and (2) the narrative of the setting in which they are acting. Foreground factors encompass (1) Christian scripture and tradition as they inform the situation, (2) theories and models drawn from the social sciences, and (3) the immediate setting and feedback from it.

He suggests three guidelines for thinking theologically about one's actions in relation to these criteria. His guidelines help to surface assumptive frameworks and convert raw experiences into remembered meanings. Carroll (1991) asks the following:

1. Do our actions enable people to enter a new relationship with God that gives renewed meaning and purpose to their lives?

2. Do our actions foster a community grounded in forgiveness, mutuality, and concern for the neighbor?

3. Do our actions empower people to live as God's people in the world?

But how are these components sequenced into some process of collaborative reflection? Osmer (1990) proposes a five-step sequence: (1) name the present action; (2) analyze why it is happening in relation to larger dynamics in the whole congregation and its social milieu; (3) relate this action to the biblical story and the church's faith; (4) decide what has been learned and what it means for how the group works; and (5) plan future actions in light of these learnings (see figure 1).

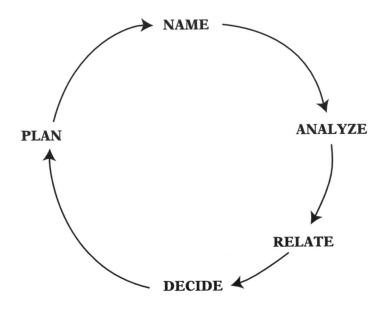

Figure 1. Five-step process for collaborative reflection

An Example of
Knowing-in-Action

Trinity Church was located in a growing community. In recent years, more and more church committees had formed, all of which sponsored programs and activities. Newly formed community groups also asked the church to provide them with space for their activities. As building usage increased, so did wear and tear on the facilities. As more groups requested space, competition increased over who controlled what rooms.

The congregation's board of trustees was responsible for coordinating usage as well as for maintaining the property. The board had traditionally performed a few clearly defined tasks: pay the insurance, keep the building in good repair, manage the memorial funds, schedule a few predictable groups for room usage. Community growth had not changed some of these tasks, such as paying the insurance and managing memorial funds. But it had made coordinating building usage much more complex and demanding.

Sue Watterson, the new chair of the trustees, knew that the trustees needed to change how they coordinated building usage, but she did not know what changes should be made. Nor did she know where to begin. After consulting with pastor Bruce Nelson, she developed a plan. Her plan included Osmer's five steps and Carroll's components.

When the new board of trustees organized during their January meeting, Sue expressed her frustration with board performance. She then invited others to share their feelings and perceptions. Most trustees admitted to problems with board performance. Agreement ended there, however. Some members felt the board's own policies and attitudes were to blame. Others felt the board was doing what it should and the problem lay with other groups and committees.

Having rehearsed a present practice about which there was concern, Sue asked board members if they would be willing to spend the next month's meeting discussing this issue. She also suggested that another trustee join her in designing this meeting. David Harris, a long-term trustee, agreed to help.

Sue understood that learning can be threatening because it sometimes challenges us to change our thinking or our behavior. By inviting the whole board to participate in designing the activities through which they might learn, Sue shifted control away from one person and gave it to the whole group. This shift reduced board members' anxiety and reduced their resistance to learning.

A few days later, Sue, David, and Bruce met to design the February meeting. "I think we should try to identify how the trustees fit into the whole congregation's recent history," Sue began.

"Maybe we could do a timeline that rehearses some congregational history. We could then see how the trustees fit into the picture," suggested Bruce.

"Let's ask them to list significant congregational practices and changes above the line and then list trustee practices and changes below the line," added David.

"But once we've done the timeline," asked Sue, "what then? Where should that take us?"

"Maybe we need to ask them to analyze the timeline, to tell how their personal stories fit into the congregation's story, and then to describe what they have learned about themselves and the congregation," Bruce replied.

In retrospect, these were two critical steps in the learning design. During the February meeting, the trustees listed many significant changes above the line. But the list below the line was virtually empty. They were able to develop a graphic, visual map that located the trustees' practices within the congregation's larger story. The timeline displayed both the congregation's story and the board's. It was also a platform from which personal stories about being a trustee and a church member could be told. As they examined the timeline, the whole board joined together in an animated discussion of the factors and forces contributing to the current situation.

"How do you think we should reflect theologically or biblically on what the trustees do," Bruce asked. "After all," he continued, "I feel like the board just sees itself as running a business. I don't think we see ourselves as stewards of an important missional resource."

"I wish I could see what I do as a ministry," David said, "Now, I just feel like I'm reviewing insurance renewals or evaluating proposals for a new boiler."

Planning theological and biblical reflection was more complicated than Bruce had expected. He wanted to avoid preaching to the trustees. They needed to explore issues and engage in active learning. Preaching would not produce this. It would take dialogue and discussion.

To facilitate active dialogue, Bruce adapted Carroll's (1991) three questions: How do the trustees add meaning to people's lives and deepen people's relationship to God? How do the trustees foster community grounded in mutuality, forgiveness, concern for neighbor? How do the trustees empower people to bear witness to their faith in the world? Bruce then prepared a brief introductory presentation, including some scripture references, that set a framework for these questions.

At the February meeting, Bruce thought he had made a terrible mistake in asking these questions. His first question was followed by a long silence. He resisted the temptation to answer it himself when everyone was silent. Using a teaching technique he had learned at a workshop, he counted to ten. This silence gave people an opportunity to collect their thoughts. When one trustee finally began to speak, others joined in. Bruce's questions elicited the trustees' mental models of the congregation. Once these privately held assumptions and perspectives were on the table, they could be examined. As they talked about these models, a shared framework for thinking and acting gradually emerged.

The meeting ended with a discussion, led by David, in which the trustees summarized what they had learned. Board members then set a future agenda to look at specific policies and procedures in light of their emerging shared mental model of trusteeship.

The planning team's design enabled the trustees to link action with reflection, faith with faithfulness. By asking questions, they slowed down the automatic processing of experience and allowed board members to examine their mental models in light of the gospel and current reality. The trustees then made new choices and decided upon alternative behaviors in light of their critical self-reflection.

The Leader's Role

While everyone on the board of trustees contributed to a learning environment, Sue's role was critical. All board members were responsible for their own learning as well as the board's collective learning. At the same time, Sue played a crucial role as facilitator. This highlights a tension inherent in a learning congregation. Everyone is responsible for creating a learning environment. Yet without someone specifically responsible for facilitating this environment, everyone's learning may be inhibited. Some individuals will always have a special responsibility for equipping people for continuous learning.

The same tension exists at the corporate level. Learning is comprehensive because everything is seen as an opportunity for people to explore meaning, clarify purposes in light of the gospel, and modify behavior on the basis of new understandings. Yet something that is everyone's responsibility runs the risk of becoming no one's responsibility. Some parts of a congregation's ministry system will always remain more responsible for learning than other parts.

How can these groups and individuals relate to other church subsystems in ways that promote learning? How can they maintain a creative tension between ministry and learning? The answer to this question explains why learning must be relational as well as comprehensive.

Relational

Learning is relational, Cremin (1976, 1989) proposes, because educational activities in one part of a system are dynamically related to all other parts of the same system. When relationships between different parts of a system go unrecognized, the whole organization's learning capacity is diminished.

Compartmentalization
Fragments Learning

A congregation's learning system can sometimes be treated as a parallel structure to its mission, ministry, or governance. The congregation has several tall, unrelated silo structures. Governance occurs in one silo. Education takes place in another. Mission and membership care happen in still others. But when an organization separates learning from its other functions, the total system will never create a learning organization. Silo-like separation of learning from other congregational functions results in fragmented learning.

It is Tuesday night at Faith Church. In the fellowship hall, a twelve-step support group begins its meeting. Members share personal narratives about their lives. Their language may include religious images and metaphors, but their speech is largely unrelated to the language of faith and scripture. Group members instead use the language of personal experience. Beyond a modest concern for the church's provision of meeting space, the group is uninterested in the congregation's governance or its other learning opportunities.

Meanwhile, in the educational wing, an evening Bible study begins its midweek class. The teacher lectures on a text's history, literary form, and other material she has gleaned from commentaries. Participants then discuss the text, but relate it neither to their own personal stories nor to larger issues in the congregation.

This same Tuesday night, the church's governing board calls its monthly meeting to order in a conference room adjacent to the sanctuary. Board members discuss budget problems, building policies, and program proposals. They use the language of problem solving and decision making. The board's deliberations determine whether the twelve-step support group will continue to use the building. They also influence what curriculum the midweek class will purchase. These discussions, however, are informed neither by the study group's biblical language nor the support group's personal language.

Although all three meetings happen in the same building on the same night, each operates independently of the others. Each meets in a different physical and social location. Each has its own specialized language. None contributes to the others' perspectives or discussions. The relational aspect of learning is conspicuously absent.

This fragmentation diminishes a congregation's capacity for learning. Congregations cultivate their learning capacity when they establish relationships between different parts of the congregation and foster conversations across functional boundaries. Cross-functional experiences can span boundaries between different congregational subsystems and prevent independent silo-like structures from developing.

Modern visitors can explore a restored Shaker village in Hancock, Massachusetts. Interpreters explain how the Shakers were a utopian religious community that emerged in the eighteenth-century. Despite their small numbers and isolated locations, Shaker communities were incredibly creative and made numerous contributions to American society: selling catalog seeds, inventing the flat broom and the clothes pin, and developing the process for making evaporated milk.

Why were the Shakers so creative? One suggested reason is their practice of rotating men and women into different farm and household chores. Men would sweep and clean; women would mow hay or milk cows. Community members who usually cooked would periodically work in the carpentry shop. Because people came to jobs with fresh perspectives, they could see beyond the narrow, routine tasks to which others had become accustomed. Because they rotated across traditional gender categories and functional areas, people could look at tasks and roles without the limitations imposed by the culturally determined mental models into which they had been socialized.

The Shakers exposed community members to different tasks and brought people from different functional areas together. This practice nurtured an incredible capacity for learning. It broke down the silo-like structures that still keep religious organizations from learning at the speed of change. It helped the Shakers build a highly creative, innovative learning organization.

Creating a Spiderweb
of Learning

Cross-functional conversations happen too infrequently in many congregations. Little (1993) proposes that a spiderweb may be the most appropriate metaphor for vital learning in congregations. A spiderweb of learning opportunities weaves together various activities and programs throughout the congregation. Planning for learning, Little urges, "necessitates an awareness of the partnership that should exist among many agencies . . . with each contributing through its unique function" (108). Building on Nelson's (1989) concept of a central planning group, she urges congregations to break out of narrow approaches and rigid structures.

A pastor in central Iowa helped his congregation to examine its practice of infant baptism (Krummel 1992). Some parents in this congregation viewed baptism as a cultural ritual, not a sacrament of God's grace. The congregation dreaded baptisms because worship was lengthened and disrupted. Although the baptismal ritual asked the congregation to affirm its responsibility for nurturing children within a community of faith, no one took any real responsibility for this task. Teaching a Sunday school class, for example, was not seen as expressing the congregation's baptismal sponsorship of children.

This pastor, using Nelson's guidelines in *How Faith Matures* (1989), formed a central study group to look at the congregation's practice of baptism. Representatives from the worship committee and the education committee, members of the governing board, and some parents met for several weeks to study baptism. This cross-functional group revealed people's mental models and assumptive frameworks about baptism. They listened to how different people and groups experienced baptism. Scripture texts were studied. Creeds and doctrinal documents were examined. Members heard how each group's actions influenced everyone else's choices.

This congregation's experience was very different from Tuesday night at Faith Church. The central study group brought together the languages of personal experience, scripture, tradition, and problem solving. They formed a cross-functional group that overcame the congregation's rigid boundaries. They moved beyond narrow, silo-like structures that had kept baptism, education, worship, and membership care unrelated to one another. The worship committee helped rework the baptismal service, involving the congregation and its governing board more fully. The education committee reframed its understanding of Christian education for children. New processes were created to stay in touch with parents of infants and toddlers. A spiderweb of learning opportunities emerged with baptism at the center.

This congregation's experience illustrates Moore's claim that learning occurs in the intersections. "This is where religious education must begin," she writes, "right in the middle, at the intersection . . . where person meets person, where person faces future, where person probes past, where person confronts contemporary issues" (1983, 110). To begin religious education elsewhere, Moore concludes, is "to split off some segment of life and artificially treat it in isolation from every other part" (111).

Relationships Between Individual, Team, and Congregational Learning

The relational context for learning is even more complex, however. A relational perspective on learning encompasses far more than how formal groups, boards, or committees relate to each other. It includes relationships between at least three different levels of learning: individual, team, and organizational. According to Watkins and Marsick, "people learn as they work together. . . . Individuals help other individuals learn. Groups learn in an almost randomly interactive fashion so that people build on one another's insights. At the organizational level, learning occurs quickly through complex interactions, as if it were a nuclear chain reaction" (1993, 9).

These three levels of learning support one another. Conversely, failure to cultivate learning at one level weakens all the others. They are like a three-legged stool. As long as all three legs are equally balanced, the stool is stable. But shorten one leg—or remove it altogether—and the stool will topple over. No amount of teaching and learning directed at a congregation's boards, councils, or committees will prove effective if individual members are not personally committed to continuous growth and learning.

A congregational culture that fails to support learning will undercut a team's learning capacity, no matter how hard the team works to learn. A culture that blames and shames people when something goes wrong will never inspire people to learn. Nothing stops learning like fear and blame. People in a shame-based culture secretly feel themselves to be inferior to others. Shame-based people will go to great extremes to deny mistakes and to cover up discrepancies. Mistakes and discrepancies serve only to confirm that one is fundamentally flawed and defective. "Shame is a matter of identity, not a behavioral infraction. There is nothing to be learned from it and no growth is opened by the experience because it only confirms one's negative feelings about oneself," according to Fossum and Mason (1986, 6). Yet, as we have seen, mistakes, discrepancies, or gaps between expectation and reality are the most basic triggers for critical reflection and learning. In a shame-based culture, no amount of emphasis on individual and team learning will translate into a learning congregation. On the other hand, a healthy congregational culture stimulates learning by treating mistakes as opportunities for growth and by actively encouraging people to explore discrepancies. Such phenomena are seen as indicators that something can be learned rather than as confirmation that someone is fundamentally flawed.

Leaders of learning congregations cultivate environments where individual, team, and congregational levels of learning are mutually supportive. But how can church leaders nurture these relationships?

Vision as a Lure
for Learning

Creating a shared vision is one way congregations can spark a creative synergy between different levels of learning. According to Marchese (1993), vision inspires people, groups, and organizations to learn. Without a vision pulling them into the future, people have little incentive to learn. A shared vision lures people to become more than they already are. It generates the energy that fuels learning. Senge proposes that "shared vision is vital for the learning organization because it provides the focus and energy for learning. While adaptive learning is possible without vision, generative learning occurs only when people are striving to accomplish something that matters deeply to them" (1990a, 206).

A clear, widely shared vision energizes church members to learn the knowledge, skills, and attitudes they need to make their vision happen. This explains why problem solving alone seldom generates energy for learning. Problem solving and management-by-objectives focus on the past and the present. Vision, on the other hand, generates its energy from the future. Vision serves as a lure drawing people toward different behaviors. People want to behave differently so they can create a different future. They are energized to learn whatever it takes to move them toward their vision. "People's natural impulse to learn is unleashed when they are engaged in an endeavor they consider worthy of their fullest commitment," states Senge (1990b, 7).

A shared vision also stimulates collaboration and team learning. A publicly known, widely shared vision encourages individuals, teams, and congregations to work together. It aligns the whole system's learning and ministering. When vision and learning are integrated, people make connections between what they already know and what they are learning, between what they are learning and what they are doing, between what they are learning and the congregation's purposes.

Congregational learning is diminished when people fail to see these relationships. When people cannot see how their particular task fits into the total vision, they lack motivation to learn (Schmidt and Finnigan 1992). This relational dimension suggests how learning is also a public activity.

Public

Learning that is relational pulls people out of private space and encourages the public processing of perceptions, judgments, and values. Individuals and teams move beyond narrowly defined private spheres and enter into a public space where they negotiate the meanings that guide their common ministries.

Public Space and Learning
Obedience to Truth

Palmer (1983) proposes that to teach is to create a free and open space where obedience to truth is practiced. We learn best, he suggests, when we enter into an open, public space where we listen to one another and negotiate shared meanings. This is similar to Evans's and Boyte's definition of public spaces. "Free spaces," they assert, "are the environments where people are able to learn self-respect, a deeper and more assertive group identity, public skills, and values of cooperation and civic virtue" (1986, 17).

Both definitions are reminiscent of Arendt's (1958) description of public space as a concrete set of learning conditions where people come together to speak, dialogue, share their stories, and struggle together within social relations that strengthen rather than weaken the possibilities for active cooperation with others. Public spaces are where we learn a language of mutuality, moral courage, and social compassion.

Educational spaces, Giroux argues, are "public spheres" centered on "critical inquiry and meaningful dialogue" (1988, 185). They create opportunities for people "to share their experiences, to work in social relations that emphasize care and concern for others, and to be introduced to forms of knowledge that provide them with the conviction and opportunity to fight for a quality of life in which all human beings benefit" (214).

Our Epistemology
Determines Our Ethic

Learning's public character, however, involves more than making private meanings public in a safe environment of critical inquiry and meaningful dialogue. Learning is public because ministry is public. Learning's public character is revealed when equipping laity for ministry in the world is linked to the church's ministry of teaching and learning. Education, according to Cremin (1976, 1989), moves inevitably from meaning formation to public action, from learning to vocation. How we come to know the world determines the way we live in it.

"Our epistemology," Palmer asserts, "is quietly transformed into our ethic" (1983, 21). The shape of our learning becomes the shape of our living. "The way we interact with the world in knowing it," he continues, "becomes the way we interact with the world as we live in it" (21). Teaching and learning involve more than thoughts or ideas. They also determine how we live with one another.

Brookfield (1987) complains that American education has forgotten that teaching and learning have public, political consequences. The speed of change has created a climate where people withdraw from public space into privatized experiences of learning and knowing. "If we feel that uncontrollable and reified forces are shaping the configuration of our individual lives, we may well retreat to the apparent security of the one sphere in which we feel some sense of control—our personal growth and relationship" (54). We focus on our inner lives, not on the public world of workplace and community. The result is an untenable relationship between learning and living. Brookfield consequently challenges educators to rediscover learning's public dimension. Educators help people to connect private lives and public issues, personal biography and social milieu. They motivate people to understand how broad, often invisible social forces construct their individual biographies.

The mental maps by which we navigate our personal lives are products of our public, social experience. They also have public, social consequences for how we relate to other people and events in our world. Just as we internalized these mental maps through learning, so we transform them through learning. As Jarvis (1992) notes, learning is a public activity involving both critique of and liberation from the culturally determined assumptive frameworks that control our lives and that sometimes cause us to collude in our own oppression.

Teaching and learning are therefore public, even prophetic, activities. The pedagogical is the political. Through learning, we sculpt the ultimate meanings that determine how we commit our time and energy to specific actions in the world.

Public Learning, Moral Courage, and Social Compassion

Hope Church is located in an affluent suburb just outside a midwestern city of 150,000. Its 500 members are well-educated, prosperous, and cosmopolitan. A number of different committees and groups collaborated in planning their Lenten programs.

First, the education committee decided to focus on urban problems in their own city. The Lenten Bible study examined Paul's missionary journeys and how early Christianity arose in an urban context. The postworship adult forum, which usually featured outside speakers discussing topical issues and current events, invited representatives from inner-city social services and ministries to describe their programs.

Second, the mission committee sponsored a series of opportunities for church members to volunteer at an inner-city soup kitchen. The junior and senior high youth groups also took turns serving meals at the same kitchen.

Third, all of Hope Church's committees took a few minutes at the beginning of their meetings to reflect on the adult forum's presentations, the Lenten Bible study, and people's experiences serving at the soup kitchen. These discussions accomplished several purposes. They made learning public because people shared their privately held assumptive frameworks about poverty, race, the city, and their church's ministry. They also facilitated comprehensive learning. Everything the church did during Lent was seen as a context for learning and dialogue. Finally, they were relational. They created a spiderweb of learning opportunities that cut across silo-like boundaries between committees and church groups.

All this happened because Carla Tirman, Hope Church's pastor, had asked the administrative council to form a central study group. This central study group, which had met during the preceding fall, was organized around the topic of the laity's ministry to the world.

After Easter, Carla and the central study group spent time working with each committee debriefing what they had learned from their Lenten experiences. These dialogues gradually coalesced into a series of action steps. A men's group organized a Cub Scout troop in one of the city's housing projects. Men who worked downtown remained afterhours as its group leaders. A women's group soon initiated a Girl Scout troop in the same housing project.

The following year, the mission committee collaborated with a congregation near the housing project to support an after-school tutoring and literacy program. Finally, the worship committee, which had initially been uninvolved in these efforts, sponsored a choral group for children living in the housing project. After a few months, someone in the choir proposed that an integrated children's choir be formed, in which the congregation's children and those from the housing project would sing together.

All these activities provided multiple opportunities for people to recognize their assumptive frameworks. In safe and free spaces, people were permitted to examine their privately held perspectives. New meanings were publicly constructed. Committees that had worked privately on their own priorities were drawn into a mutual ministry undergirded by a shared vision.

Church leaders and educators have sometimes treated teaching and learning as activities that happen apart from public space—in the private, sacred realm of church and family. The result is a Christian education that lacks both critique and liberation. A key challenge for leaders of learning congregations is to create ways for people to move from being isolated consumers of information toward becoming a community of learners who together construct frameworks of meaning and ministry that are publicly shared, critical, and liberating.

4

Leading at the Speed
of Change

How can church leaders cultivate learning that is comprehensive, relational, and public? How can they equip a people of God for individual, team, and congregational learning? Two basic characteristics distinguish the leaders of learning congregations. First, they themselves are learners. They model what it means to learn at the speed of change. They cannot challenge others to learn if they are not learning, growing, and changing. Second, they foster opportunities for the whole people of God to clarify their vision, to examine their assumptive frameworks, and to construct more flexible, fluid, and apt mental models that express people's deepest Christian convictions.

A DIFFERENT VISION
OF LEADERSHIP

This description differs significantly from how people usually define leadership. Good leaders traditionally are responsible for planning, directing, controlling, and evaluating an organization's activities. They are expected to have more knowledge and expertise than their subordinates. They are to know what is happening, to take charge when situations are uncertain, and to solve every problem.

The Failure of
Traditional Leadership

Bradford and Cohen (1987) associate these characteristics with what they call *heroic leadership*. Heroic leaders, according to Bradford and Cohen, sit atop organizational pyramids. They control the information, make the strategic decisions, and evaluate how others implement their plans. These leaders have become dysfunctional in today's permanent white-water society. Three dynamics explain why heroic leadership undermines individual, team, and organizational learning.

Problems with
Heroic Leadership

First, heroic leaders try to know and do everything. Because all communication is centralized in the leader, information does not flow easily or freely. Feedback on performance moves slowly up the organizational ladder. It takes just as long for a decision to filter downward to those responsible for implementation. Since information and feedback are crucial to learning, whatever limits them also limits learning.

Second, heroic leaders create organizational cultures where they alone are responsible for the system's performance. They overfunction on behalf of everyone else. Consequently, no one else feels responsible for the organization's total performance. People are free to focus on narrowly defined tasks and immediate responsibilities. They identify with their committee, board, or department rather than with the whole congregation. Narrow, nonchallenging tasks do not stimulate people to reflect on their actions, however. Nor are people challenged to think systemicly or complexly when they identify only with their own position or project.

Third, heroic leaders are kept busy with routine tasks. Routine work drives out nonroutine work. The urgent replaces the important. No time is left to build a shared vision or to align people with this vision. Without a shared vision, it is virtually impossible to spin a spiderweb of related learning activities throughout an organization. Without a shared vision, people are not energized to learn the knowledge, skills, and values needed to realize their collective goals.

Heroic leaders reap some short-term satisfactions. They enjoy the illusion that they are irreplaceable. They benefit from feeling more important than others. They experience a rush of success when they solve a problem all by themselves. But ultimately "the short-lived pleasure of personally solving a particular problem is less satisfying than seeing others grow in competence and the [whole organization] perform at a higher level" (Bradford and Cohen 1987, 273).

Heroic leadership can fulfill the leader's own need to feel important and in control. It can also satisfy the needs of constituents who would rather have the leader do the hard work of adaptive change instead of doing it themselves. Heifetz, on the other hand, has noted that exercising leadership often means going against the grain of what people want and expect:

> Rather than fulfilling the expectation for answers, one provides questions; rather than protecting people from outside threat, one lets people feel the threat in order to stimulate adaptation; instead of orienting people to their current roles, one disorients people so that new role relationships develop; rather than quelling conflict, one generates it; instead of maintaining norms, one challenges them. (1994, 126)

Exercising leadership means engaging people to make progress on the adaptive challenges facing them in a permanent whitewater society. Such progress requires learning. And leadership means sculpting the learning process so that the level of distress people experience is neither too great nor too little, so that attention is kept on the adaptive challenge rather than on side issues or personalities, and so that the people themselves are given the adaptive challenge to resolve the issue rather than shift the burden for a solution onto the leader. When those exercising church leadership can perform these tasks, they have avoided the pitfall of heroic leadership.

Saul and Heroic Leadership

An awareness of the limitations of heroic leadership is nothing new. Israel's history is littered with examples of its failure. Saul, Israel's very first king, provides a dramatic illustration.

Having grown weary of being responsible for Israel's common life, all the elders gathered together and came to Samuel at Ramah. They requested, "Appoint for us, then, a king to govern us." Above all else, they wanted a heroic leader: "We are determined to have a king over us, so that . . . our king may govern us and go out before us and fight our battles" (1 Sam. 8:19–20). They wanted a leader who would be responsible for everything, who would take charge and solve all their problems for them. Saul even looked the part. He was young, handsome, and held in honor. Best of all, "whatever he says always comes true" (1 Sam. 9:6).

But the burdens of heroic leadership eventually destroyed Saul and swept Israel into a national crisis. Since everything was centralized in Saul, less and less information flowed freely to and around him. Gradually, this lack of information impaired his judgment. He made unlawful sacrifices (1 Sam. 13:8–15). He committed himself to a rash oath that he later regretted (1 Samuel 14). He so overfunctioned for the whole people that he eventually became suspicious of anyone else's ideas, gifts, accomplishments. Eventually these failings accumulated into such a crushing weight that Saul drifted into madness and a destructive civil war with David. Only Saul's military defeat and eventual suicide ended the cycle of destruction.

Jesus and
Adaptive Leadership

By contrast, Jesus understood what it meant to walk the razor's edge of adaptive leadership. When the people asked for authoritative answers, he responded by asking questions. When asked whether it was lawful to pay taxes to the emperor, Jesus responded by asking a question: Whose head is on the coin? (Matt. 22:15–22). When asked to answer by whose authority he healed and taught, Jesus responded not by giving an answer but by asking a question: Did the baptism of John come from heaven or was it of human origin? (Matt. 21:23–27).

Instead of maintaining norms, Jesus challenged them. He healed on the sabbath (Matt. 12:9–14). He broke the norms of clean and unclean by eating and drinking with sinners (Matt. 11:18–19). Rather than orient people to their current roles and relationships, Jesus unsettled the rigid roles of men and women

(Luke 8:1–3; John 4:4–42) and created the conditions where the old barriers between Greek and Jew, slave and free, male and female were transcended. He understood how to create a holding environment (Kegan 1982) that could simultaneously challenge and support people as they learned new behaviors and values. He could support those who were heavily burdened and seeking rest, yet also challenge them to bear much fruit, for the fields were white unto harvest.

Shaping Meaning in a Community of Shared Practice

Exercising leadership within Christian communities of faith does not mean that one must make all the decisions, solve all the problems, or control what everyone else does. Church leaders are called to model their leadership after Jesus rather than Saul. They are to engage people in making progress on the adaptive challenges they face in a permanent white-water society. They collaborate with people in shaping and reshaping meaning within a community of shared practice. They develop people, not plans. They exercise the gift of discernment, not deciding. Instead of controlling people and communities, these leaders equip individuals and communities to expand continually their capacity to clarify purposes, to explore mental models, and to understand complexity. These leaders are educators who cultivate communities where people build shared meaning and learn new knowledge, skills, and values that can improve the common good.

While Paul is sometimes perceived as a rigid and authoritarian leader, his letters suggest he was more interested in coordination than in control, that he understood ministry as helping the people of God shape and reshape meaning in a community of shared ministry. Paul refuses to command Philemon to return Onesimus. Instead he wants Philemon to act on the basis of mutuality and a shared relationship in Christ: "Though I am bold enough in Christ to command you to do your duty, yet I would rather appeal to you on the basis of love" (Philemon 8).

Paul's introduction to the letter to the Romans reflects his attraction to heroic leadership and his struggle against it. "For I am longing to see you so that I may share with you some spiritual gift to strengthen you," he writes (Rom. 1:11). Then he catches himself practically in midsentence and corrects himself: "or rather so that we may be mutually encouraged by each other's faith, both yours and mine" (Rom. 1:12).

THE PASTOR AS EDUCATOR

Some congregations and pastors are still caught in patterns of heroic leadership. Denominational polities and church bylaws sometimes describe the pastor as the congregation's chief administrative officer. Pastors occasionally overfunction for their congregations, trying to solve every problem, answer every question, be responsible for everything that happens.

Ministry is thereby reduced to whatever the pastor does. Laity are either recipients of pastoral services or workers who carry out their pastor's orders. Church members are not expected to learn or grow. They are thus deprived of the experiences in ministry that could shape their sense of vocation and form their understanding of Christian faith. Fishburn (1988) complains that pastors spend far too much time on pastoral care and not enough time teaching. Conversely, laity spend far too little time on pastoral care and are then left to staff the church's educational program with almost no pastoral support, direction, or guidance. A number of factors contribute to this neglect of teaching and learning. Some are historical and cultural. Others are theological, rooted in the ecclesiologies that inform our perspectives on church and ministry.

The Sunday School and the
Disappearance of Pastors as Educators

Fishburn (1988) believes that historical trends explain why teaching and learning are low priorities in some congregations. She also offers a proposal for recovering teaching and learning as important disciplines within the church.

Two Parallel Structures

According to Fishburn (1988), the Sunday school's emergence, development, and decline accounts for the disappearance of the pastor as an educational leader. It also explains why some contemporary congregations neglect teaching and learning.

During the nineteenth century, the Sunday school acquired almost total responsibility for religious education. Since the Sunday school was a lay-led institution, the pastor's role as an educator became marginalized and slowly faded away.

In time, two parallel structures evolved. The church at worship was led by a theologically educated pastor and governed by pastorally trained officers. The lay-dominated Sunday school was responsible for congregational education (Lynn and Wright 1980). This parallel structure was enshrined in bricks and budgets. The church and the Sunday school had separate treasurers, budgets, and offering envelopes. An educational "wing"—or even a separate building—housed the Sunday school, setting it apart from the sanctuary where the church worshiped.

The Sunday school provided more than education for all ages. It was a learning laboratory where future leaders were trained. It also encouraged the nurture of lay leadership and lay ministry. In addition, it had important fellowship, mission, and evangelism functions (Lynn and Wright 1980). This structure left pastors with no specific educational responsibilities, however. So they gradually ceased to be "expected to give leadership to educational activities, mission activities, teacher training, or leadership training" (Fishburn 1988, 198).

Unfortunately, the Sunday school has steadily declined in numbers and importance since the 1960s. Consequently, a vacuum in educational leadership has developed. Pastors long ago stopped educating and training church members. With the Sunday school's demise, its lay-lead processes for leadership training and development have also collapsed. "Because of the history of the two leadership structures," writes Fishburn, "it is unusual to find a congregation where there is evidence that the recruitment, training, and support of many forms of lay ministry are important to anyone" (1988, 201).

Linking Learning to Ministry

Fishburn proposes that pastors can best reclaim their historic responsibility for teaching and learning by integrating these tasks into equipping laity for ministry. This requires two types of learning opportunities, she suggests. The first is formal instruction. The second involves learning through doing ministry. It might also be called practical theological reflection or knowing-in-action.

This second context for learning is frequently overlooked, however. In several congregations where I served as pastor, the number of adults enrolled in formal Christian education was dwarfed by the numbers engaged in ministry. The most active members spent several hours each week in ministry activities or church meetings. They were in weekly worship or Christian education for no more than one-and-a-half hours.

Which activities ultimately equipped these laity to make sense of Christian faith? Which had a greater impact on their beliefs and actions? I seldom had people leave the church because they heard something offensive in a church school class. But people frequently became angry and left because something happened to them in a church meeting. This alone suggests how powerfully church meetings and ministry experiences can touch people's lives and transform their faith.

We sometimes forget that experiences in ministry shape how people make sense of Christian faith. People's everyday experiences in their homes, workplaces, and communities are frequently neglected as learning opportunities. These experiences represent rich possibilities for practical theological reflection, particularly when they are regarded as the primary context for the laity's ministry.

Just as we occasionally assume that people are not engaged in ministry if they are not involved in "church work," we sometimes infer that people are not learning about the Christian faith if they are not in formal educational settings. Yet, as Tough (1979) discovered in his research on adult learning projects, most adults can describe one or more learning projects they intentionally undertake each year. These projects usually occur informally, episodically, and independently. They are also closely linked to work or leisure activities. Adults learn in order to accomplish something they either must do or want to do. Their learning is instrumental. Adults learn by solving problems or by accomplishing task-related goals.

Could the same be true for church members? Annual statistical reports typically count those participating in formal, short-term or long-term classes in order to measure how many people are engaged in Christian education. This calculation, however, overlooks those who are informally learning as they plan for and engage in ministry. What would happen if our yearly statistical reports asked church leaders to document how many members were learning through experiences in ministry?

The ministry of the laity is a rich resource for educating people *for* ministry *through* ministry. The current separation of Bible study and prayer from "church work" is the legacy of the Sunday school's parallel structure. Fishburn (1988) calls for the Bible, prayer, and Christian reflection to be reintegrated with church work, linking faith with faithfulness, action with reflection. Church leaders foster learning that is public when they cultivate the laity's ministry in the world as critical content for practical theological reflection. The learning congregation, built around a renewed ministry of teaching and learning, equips the laity for their proper role as those who bear public witness to the gospel in their daily lives and work.

A Pastoral Ecclesiology
or a Teaching Ecclesiology?

Osmer (1993) also attempts to account for the chasm that has developed between the pastor's role in governance and his or her educational responsibilities. He describes the problem theologically rather than historically.

Over the past few decades, pastors and congregations have embraced what he calls a *pastoral ecclesiology*. By a pastoral ecclesiology, Osmer means "an understanding of the church in which the congregation is viewed primarily as a supportive, nurturing community that assists people in times of crisis and forms programs to meet their needs" (1993, 128). Nothing captures the essence of pastoral ecclesiology better than the phrase "meeting people's needs." Congregations with this ecclesiology organize their ministry around the felt needs of members or prospective members.

Church leaders, consequently, become either managers or therapists. As managers, leaders adopt a passive, process-oriented role. They help church groups reach their own decisions or assist them in their program planning and implementation. As therapists, church leaders limit themselves to helping others express their feelings or explore their own values. As a result, Osmer complains, church leaders "are less the mediators of an authoritative, potentially disclosive tradition than the facilitators of social and psychological processes" (1993, 129).

Such ministry does little to help church members distinguish between their own felt needs or culturally shaped values and the gospel's radical claim upon their lives. More important, it reverses the basic pattern of response to God found throughout scripture. According to the biblical pattern, people come to God in order to discover their true needs and respond to them. In scripture, the felt needs of people do not set the church's agenda for ministry.

Osmer counters this pastoral ecclesiology with his own alternative ecclesiological vision. His "teaching ecclesiology" views the church as a schoolhouse of faith, where people "come to learn what they do not already know, where ongoing growth and struggle are expected, where a determinate subject matter stands at the center of what is taught" (1993, 130). Instead of organizing ministry around people's felt needs, the congregation derives a normative vision of the Christian life from God's self-disclosure in Jesus Christ and then "provides its members with a course of study by which they can make that vision their own over the course of their lives" (130).

Like Fishburn, Osmer adopts a two-pronged emphasis on both formal and informal learning opportunities. A spiderweb of formal and informal educational opportunities is spun across the congregation, making learning both relational and comprehensive.

Congregations, Osmer writes, must "take more seriously the importance of ongoing, consistent education during the week. It is simply not possible to teach the amount of information and foster the kind of personal appropriation that needs to take place during one hour on Sunday morning" (1993, 134).

People's experiences in ministry are an equally powerful learning opportunity. Consistent participation in action/reflection experiences, Osmer continues, might keep congregations from becoming self-absorbed communities, sealed off from the surrounding culture. It is imperative, he says, to link participation in ministry "with educational processes that allow people to reflect on what they are experiencing: to share the feelings that are stirred up, to pray and read scripture, and to study the broader social forces that impact the people with whom they are working" (1993, 137). The more learning becomes public,

Osmer hints, the more it remains comprehensive and relational.

Leadership as an Educational Activity

As the church seeks to minister in a permanent white-water society, Christians struggle to learn at the speed of change. In this context, church leaders are called to exercise their responsibilities in new ways. Cultivating opportunities for Christians to learn eclipses facilitating social and psychological processes. A teaching ministry that builds the congregation's learning capacity replaces a heroic ministry that makes all decisions and directs all activities.

Church leaders too frequently feel they have provided adequate learning opportunities when they recruit church school teachers, sponsor new classes, or teach another midweek Bible study. Leading at the speed of change requires more.

Leading is an educational task as well as a practical one. When individuals, teams, and congregations make decisions, solve problems, or plan for the future, they are learning. Assumptive worlds are revealed, challenged, and critiqued. Complex thinking is fostered. New experiences are transformed into meaning even as prior frameworks of meaning are searched and revised. Christian faith and tradition are probed for new insights.

Church leaders sometimes do not discern this relationship between leading and learning. They focus so intently on what they are doing that they miss the educational opportunities inherent in how they are doing it. Yet it is through such opportunities that leaders shape and reshape meaning in a community of shared practice. When this happens, church leaders have moved beyond facilitating social and psychological processes. They are shaping and reshaping meaning in a community of faithful practice.

HOW DO WE BEGIN AND WHAT DO WE DO?

Where do pastors and educators start when they want to lead at the speed of change? The first step is to begin with themselves. "Leaders are, first of all, learners and teachers," asserts Jones (1993, 47). Ultimately, all leadership begins with self-leadership. "It is one thing for leaders to call for change and to attempt to direct the change. It is another thing for leaders to see that the primary change called for is a change in themselves . . . and in the ways they lead," Jones proposes (57).

Becoming a Learner—The Choice of Self-Leadership

According to Friedman (1985), effective leaders are characterized by self-differentiation. They change their organizations by changing themselves. Steinke uses Lewin's formula to explain this approach. Behavior (b) is a result of the transaction (f) between personality (p) and environment (e): $b = f(p \times e)$ "We can change the person and the environment changes, and we can change the environment and the person changes. Person and context are mutual influences. They form a system," Steinke explains (1993, 91).

We usually initiate change by beginning out there. We want to change the context around us. We mistakenly begin with the e variable in Lewin's formula. We complain about what is wrong with other people and demand that they change. We focus on others and what they ought to do, ignoring what we can do to change ourselves.

Steinke (1993) and Friedman (1985) challenge leaders to begin with themselves. Since person and context are interdependent parts of one system, a change in one component alters the other. If the leader changes, the whole context changes.

Jesus speaks of removing the log from one's own eye before pointing to the speck of dirt in another's eye. "Why do you see the speck in your neighbor's eye, but do not notice the log in your own eye? Or how can you say to your neighbor, 'Let me take the speck out of your eye,' while the log is in your own eye?" (Matt. 7:3–4). Similarly, we need to begin by changing ourselves rather than by demanding that others change. Look at what we ourselves can learn and do differently, Jesus says, before we command others to act or think differently. Ultimately, all we can ever really change is ourselves. We cannot force others to change. Change is a choice each person makes. Leaders cannot motivate other people. They can only create the conditions under which people may motivate themselves.

When we begin with self-leadership, we start by changing ourselves. We accept the discipline of learning, growing, and changing. This alters the whole system of which we are a part. It initiates changes elsewhere in our context. Since leaders are one of the most important parts of an organizational system, the whole system changes when the leader changes. Becoming a learner, therefore, is the first and most important step leaders can take if they wish to cultivate a learning congregation.

Designing Learning Environments

The leader's second task is to design learning environments where people can think more complexly, examine their assumptive worlds, and develop shared frameworks of meaning capable of forming and informing the church's ministry. Watkins and Marsick (1993) identify six action steps that cultivate individual, team, and organizational learning:

1. create continuous learning opportunities
2. promote inquiry and dialogue
3. encourage collaboration and team learning
4. establish systems to capture and share learning
5. empower people toward a collective vision
6. connect the organization to its environment

Continuous Learning

People learn continually, according to Watkins and Marsick (1993), when they have ample opportunities for knowing-in-action as well as easy access to formal study. Neither formal study nor knowing-in-action happen automatically, however. People need particular skills, knowledge, and values in order to learn continually.

Dialogue and Inquiry

The disciplines of dialogue and mutual inquiry facilitate both knowing-in-action and formal learning. Dialogue, Vella

(1994) asserts, is at the heart of learning. But dialogue itself is an acquired skill, it does not come naturally.

Collaboration

Dialogue and inquiry suggest collaboration with other people. Without conversation partners, there can be no dialogue. Learning is highly social. We learn best when we learn together.

Administrators at a large private university were concerned about the high failure rate in their calculus course. Administrators wanted to understand the factors predicting success so they could better advise students for whom calculus was a required course. Researchers studied a number of possible variables. They found that the best predictor of success was not the number of math courses a student had already taken. Nor were students' SAT scores or college GPA useful in predicting who would succeed. Not even the student's IQ was a reliable predictor. Much to the researchers' surprise, participation in a study group was the key variable.

When people collaborate as part of a team, they learn together. They do not rely on an expert to tell them what they need. Together they determine the meaning of their activities and create shared mental models. They form a community of teaching and learning.

Shared Vision

Leaders facilitate learning when they help people create a shared vision. The motivation to learn, Watkins and Marsick (1993) propose, arises from more than a desire to solve current problems or to adapt to present conditions. People are motivated to learn when they are future-oriented. As Marchese (1993) observes, a shared vision shifts the impetus for learning from the present to the future, increasing the motivation and willingness to learn. When people collectively develop a shared vision, they are motivated to learn the knowledge, skills, and values needed to accomplish it.

Capturing and Sharing Knowledge

Leaders help organizations learn from their history, environment, and performance. But the whole system must capture and store what is learned so it is available for future retrieval. I was working on my word processor one evening long past when my efforts were productive. Tired and hungry, I rushed to finish and inadvertently turned off the machine without saving my document. I lost several hours of hard work because I did not save and store my text. All human systems—individuals, teams, and even whole organizations—are like a word processor. If new knowledge, skills, and values are not stored so that they can be retrieved for future use, they are lost and quickly forgotten.

Connecting to the Larger Environment

Leaders of learning congregations know that congregations do not exist for their own sake but for the sake of ministry. They do not foster learning so that people can enjoy some narcissistic self-absorption. Congregations cultivate learning environments so that people are better equipped to live as Christ's disciples, bearing witness to the good news in the larger world. "The essence of the Church," Barth contends, "is the event in which the community is a light shining also in the world. . . . The Church does not exist by pondering, studying, discussing, and preparing itself for this relationship to the world. The Church exists in actually accomplishing this relationship" (1964, 66).

Some action steps are clearly more appropriate for cultivating congregational learning than for fostering individual or team learning. A few strategies (providing continual formal and informal learning opportunities or promoting dialogue and inquiry) clearly target individual learners. Other strategies (building shared vision, capturing and sharing newly learned adaptive behaviors, or connecting the congregation to its environment) obviously are designed for congregational systems. Similarly, one can immediately link collaboration to strategies for team learning.

At the same time, congregations are a system, and whenever you touch one part of a system, you touch all other parts as well. When one adopts a strategy to improve individual learning, it also has consequences for team and congregational learning. When church leaders work to improve collaboration in teams,

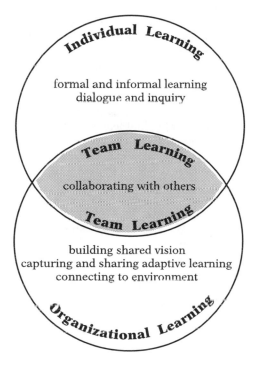

Figure 2: Relationship of individual, team, and organizational learning

it will impact the congregation's capacity for organizational learning, as well as enhance the learning of individuals.

Figure 2 illustrates the interactive relationship between individual, team, and organizational learning. The overlapping circles represent the interpenetrating dynamic of these strategies for learning. Strategies appropriate for individual and organizational learning are listed within their respective circles. A strategy has its primary effect at its own level, but its secondary effects extend to the other levels. Actions that promote learning at one level reverberate through the remaining ones, just as a pebble dropped into a pond creates waves that spread outward, until they wash against the most distant shore. A strategy to enhance individual learning will influence the congregation's capacity for

organizational learning. Conversely, a strategy to cultivate organizational learning has consequences for individual learning.
The two circles hence overlap.

Team learning is located at the intersection of individual and
organizational learning. Collaboration skills work downward
into organizational learning. You cannot build a shared vision
without team collaboration, for example. Similarly, collaboration
skills work upward to individual learning. Dialogue and mutual
inquiry remain impossible when people lack collaborative tools
and strategies. Thus, when one looks at the diagram, one can see
that as a strategy moves closer to the overlapping area between
individual and organizational learning, it is based more on team
learning. As it moves farther away from the team learning sector
where individual and organizational learning intersect, the less it
involves team-related skills. Building a shared vision, for example, clearly requires more collaborative learning than does connecting the congregation to the larger environment. Dialogue and
mutual inquiry involve more team-related skills than does knowing-in-action. Team learning thus retains some characteristics of
both individual learning and organizational learning, yet it can
also be isolated as a discrete type of learning.

This diagram also explains why actions by church leaders
sometimes have unanticipated consequences. Church leaders
may decide to engage the congregation in building a shared vision. But this same intervention unexpectedly motivates church
members to take advantage of the congregation's formal and informal opportunities for individual learning.

Church leaders who hope to cultivate learning congregations can thus begin at any of three points: individual, team, or
the organizational system itself. At the same time, leaders must
remind themselves that no matter what level they enter into the
process, their actions will also have consequences at the remaining two.

In one congregation, leaders might begin at the individual
level, encouraging continual formal and informal opportunities
for learning. They are simultaneously fostering conditions that
improve team and congregational learning, preparing church
members for future interventions at these levels. In another congregation, leaders may find it easier to begin at the organizational level, connecting the congregation to the larger environment and creating a shared vision. This shared vision then

stimulates learning as people are motivated to acquire the knowledge, skills, and abilities necessary to realize their vision.

In still other congregations, leaders may find an opening for generative learning at the team level where they can encourage collaboration. Leaders then build on these collaborative skills to develop a shared vision and to motivate individual learning. Team-level strategies are usually the most powerful ones because collaborative skills are fundamental to one's ability to engage in dialogue and inquiry. They also determine one's capacity to participate in the public process associated with building a shared vision. It is for this reason that team learning is described as operating at the intersection of individual and organizational learning.

A Larger Vision

These six action steps or strategies can cultivate learning that is public, comprehensive, and relational. By encouraging collaboration and team learning, leaders promote learning that is relational. They cultivate learning that is comprehensive when they equip church members to reflect on the knowing-in-action that happens as they engage in ministry and mission. They facilitate learning that is public as they connect the congregation and its members to the larger environment, making people's ministry in the world the content for practical theological reflection.

Ultimately, all six strategies are embedded in a larger vision of congregations as communities that foster individual learning, that facilitate team learning, and that cultivate congregational learning. Part 2 of this book describes specific strategies to implement individual, team, and congregational learning.

Part 2

LEADING THE LEARNING CONGREGATION

5

Fostering Individual Learning

Individual, team, and congregational learning, as we have already noted, form one interdependent system. It is impossible to touch one without simultaneously touching the others. Nonetheless, it is sometimes necessary to isolate one of these levels for purposes of analysis and strategic reflection. This chapter will focus on the strategies, skills, and tools important for individual learning. The next chapter will discuss how best to address the second level of learning in our model: team learning. The following chapter will explore congregational learning.

At least two fundamental strategies promote individual learning: (1) having the skills and tools necessary to learn continually from one's own experience, and (2) being able to engage in dialogue and inquiry.

CONTINUAL EXPERIENTIAL LEARNING

Having experiences is not the same as learning. We may learn the wrong thing from an experience. Worse still, our response may block learning. Whether in a classroom or a committee meeting, how we react to a situation determines what we learn from it. Jarvis (1992) identifies several ways people respond to potential learning situations. Some responses foster growth. Others do not. Church leaders encourage continual learning when they understand these differences, minimize nonlearning responses, and maximize those situations most likely to cultivate continual learning.

Jarvis's (1992) analysis of nonlearning responses is particularly relevant to church leaders. His nonlearning responses include preventive, anomic, alienating, and presumptive responses to potential learning situations. As church leaders better understand these responses, they can minimize the factors that block learning. Equally important is Jarvis's analysis of how people can respond creatively and positively to potential learning experiences.

Preventive Responses

Group pressures and social taboos can prevent people from learning. Jarvis (1992) describes this as a preventive response to a potential learning situation. People want to learn but are prevented from doing so.

Jackie felt that God called her to ministry. But her pastor discouraged her from exploring this call, telling her that God never called women to the ordained ministry. Jackie's pastor prevented her from exploring the meaning of her experience. Juan's seven-year-old daughter died of leukemia. Why would God let this happen, he wondered. But he never felt comfortable sharing his doubts at church. He knew members of his Sunday school class would tell him that God works for good in all things. He worried that his pastor would remind him to praise God no matter what happens. Because group pressure prevented Juan from exploring the meaning of his daughter's death, he was deprived of an opportunity to deepen his faith.

Brueggemann proposes that "we are accustomed to think that there is some match-up between the substance of truth and the structures of authority" (1982, 44). The stable ordering of society depends on our willingness to credit the authorities with having access to reliable information and dependable truths. The Hebrew prophets did not take this official version of truth too seriously, however. Neither should we. "Knowledge for the crisis," Brueggemann says, "is not given in normal channels and by regular means. . . . There is no reliable one-to-one correlation between the structures of society and the in-breaking of new truth from God" (43).

In Genesis 41, Pharaoh's royal apparatus cannot provide the interpretive key to unlock his dream's meaning. Only a Hebrew prisoner languishing in jail on false charges possesses the wisdom to understand its symbolism. In Exodus 8, the imperial technicians cannot do what Hebrew slaves easily perform. Centuries later in Jerusalem, King Zedekiah visits an imprisoned Jeremiah because the prophet knows what the king and his court do not (Jeremiah 38).

The royal task is always to assure continuity. Kings and queens rely on the consensus that this world is the only one we have had and the only one we will ever have. They reign by virtue of group pressures and cultural taboos that keep difficult questions from being asked. The Hebrew prophets challenged this royal consensus of meaning. Church leaders, likewise, should not be too easily seduced into a royal consciousness. They are called to cultivate environments where alternative voices are heard and unspoken questions are asked, where God's poetic, prophetic imagination breaks through the existing consensus of meaning and illumines an alternative interpretation of experience.

Paul's advice in 1 Corinthians 14:26–33 provides a useful guide for church leaders who want to minimize preventive responses (Yoder 1992). Paul is instructing the Corinthians on how to hold a church meeting in the power of the Spirit. Whoever has something to say, something given by the Spirit, can have the floor. Others are instructed to yield the floor and listen. The only limitation is that the meeting be moderated so that the conversation remains orderly. Christians learn and grow when they are part of a free, open conversation in which no one is prevented from sharing their experience. Yoder refers to this as "the Rule of Paul" and advocates open conversation as a basic ecclesial practice through which decision making and learning occur.

According to Palmer (1983), hospitable space makes learning possible. When people are pressured by group norms or prevented by social taboos, they are not in safe, hospitable space. Hospitable space is safe space. Vella describes some of the conditions promoting safety: affirmation, listening, attention to feelings as well as words, respect, accountability to learners. "Safety," she writes, "can be felt in a learning situation. These are the signs: laughter, a certain ease and camaraderie, a flow of questions from the learners, the teacher's invitation for comments on the process" (1994, 181).

Anomic Responses

An anomic response occurs when the gap between our framework of meaning and a new experience is so great that we withdraw into private space. Meaningful learning cannot take place under such conditions. Anomic responses happen when church members confront situations that are too overwhelming or too threatening.

Lois Alexander volunteered to go on a church-sponsored mission trip to Haiti. The trip had a two-fold purpose: to build a medical clinic and to educate middle-class North Americans about Third World issues. Lois's encounter with poverty and disease overwhelmed her orderly middle-class assumptions. Although she worked with others to build a small medical clinic, she mentally withdrew into a private, inner world. In the end, her trip confirmed rather than transformed her prejudices against people of color.

People cannot learn when they feel threatened and overwhelmed. Learning requires safety. Safety, Vella believes, "does not obviate the natural challenge of learning" nor does it "take away any of the hard work involved in learning" (1994, 6). But when people are threatened and afraid, they are under too much stress to learn. Walton (1969) proposes that people must experience some stress—some disjuncture between what they already know or believe and what they are experiencing—if they are to learn. If this stress becomes too great, they shut down and cannot learn. Up to a certain point, learning increases as stress increases. After this point, learning drops off rapidly.

The challenge is to create enough stress for people to learn but not so much that they become overwhelmed and withdraw into private space. Sequencing the learning task from simple to complex, from nonthreatening to challenging, from group-supported to solo performance is one way to manage learners' stress and to minimize anomic responses. "When you, as a teacher, see fear, confusion, reluctance to try in the learner," Vella advises, "test the sequence of the learning task. You may find you have not honored their need for small steps between tasks" (1994, 9).

In essence, those who exercise leadership create a holding environment in which learning and adaptive work can occur.

Heifetz (1994) uses the analogy of a pressure cooker to describe this process: Too much heat and the pot explodes. Not enough heat and the meal will not cook. Leaders must gauge how to regulate the pressure based on three broad determinants: (1) the severity of the adaptive challenge and the stress it generates, (2) the resilience of those doing the work and their support system, and (3) the strength of the holding environment itself. Monitoring the relationship between these three variables is crucial for those attempting to exercise adaptive, educative leadership.

Like Lois Alexander, Steve Hardaker also went on a short-term mission to Haiti. Steve had a different experience, however. Steve's team leader required volunteers to attend several days of orientation before they left. On the first afternoon, participants shared their personal journeys and joined in trust-building exercises. This created the psychological safety to share deeply held opinions and feelings.

The team next participated in a series of role plays. The leader carefully planned these exercises, beginning with simple, nonthreatening situations: talking to a Haitian carpenter who was helping to build the clinic or accepting a gift from a Haitian host family. He gradually introduced more challenging exercises: meeting a beggar on the street or comforting a mother whose child has just died of a preventable childhood disease.

Participants debriefed each exercise and shared their feelings, thoughts, or reflections. The leader skillfully wove information about economic, political, and social problems into these discussions. When the mission team finally arrived in Haiti, Steve was far better prepared than Lois to learn from his experiences.

Alienating Responses

Alienating responses occur when we learn from an experience but, in the process, are alienated from ourselves, from the subject of our learning, or from both (Jarvis 1992). Carlos was brought up in a strict religious environment. He went to church twice on Sunday and once on Wednesday. He memorized the Westminster Confession and major sections of the Bible to please his parents and Sunday school teachers. Carlos transformed his experiences into meaning, but he also became alienated. He stopped worshiping as soon as he went away to college. Twenty years later, Carlos still remains hostile to organized religion.

People are less likely to become alienated when they feel in control of their own learning. Vella calls this the principle of respect for learners. "Engaging adults in their own learning," she proposes, "means engaging them as subjects of that learning. As far as possible, they make decisions on what and how they will learn" (1994, 13). According to Bradford and Cohen, most people will not change how they think or behave when the power discrepancy between their leaders and themselves "increases beyond conditions of interdependence to dependence. When people feel that they have some control over what will happen to them, they are more willing to be open to influence" (1987, 164).

Ironically, the more church leaders emphasize their power and expertise, the more they create barriers to learning. Such leaders treat laity as objects of someone else's action rather than as subjects of their own learning. This almost inevitably produces an alienating response. Carroll (1991) observes that a pastor's cultural authority usually exceeds his or her social authority. Social authority refers to the capacity to control or to coerce another person's behavior or thought. Cultural authority, on the other hand, involves influencing beliefs, shaping perceptions, affecting how people define reality.

Many pastors, trapped in traditional paradigms of church and ministry, assume social authority to coerce. "At one time," Carroll reminds his readers, "clergy had the power of excommunication, and congregations had the power of expulsion" (1991, 39). We now live in a pluralistic, democratic society where the church is a voluntary association. As a result, pastoral authority is primarily cultural rather than social. "When a pastor preaches, teaches, or counsels, she may be less interested in controlling or influencing behavior than in influencing how the others think about an issue. . . . The primary intent is shaping the others' perspective" (38).

Church leaders are less likely to evoke alienating responses when they treat others as the subjects of their own learning. These leaders invite church members into a collaborative contract where they reflect together on the meaning of experience. "They join," Carroll proposes, "in a mutual effort to understand

and find solutions to the issues confronting [them]" (1991, 132). Church leaders "treat the others not as dependent clients but as people who bring their own insights, gifts, and reflective capacities to the setting" (133).

Presumptive Responses

When people operate by habit, they do not reflect on their experience. Jarvis (1992) describes this as a presumptive response. According to Russo and Schoemaker (1989), the right way to play golf goes against habitual ways of acting. Most beginners think they should bend their arm, for example. Similarly, learning often requires people to go against habitual patterns of thinking and acting.

Members of the Seek and Sow Sunday school class have been meeting together for twenty years. Members arrive early to have coffee and doughnuts. After moving to their chairs, they discuss the week's events and invite prayer requests. They take turns reading aloud the lesson in their study booklet. They next read the questions at the end of the lesson, responding with brief, conventional answers. The class finally dismisses with a prayer as members leave for worship. The Seek and Sow class serves to confirm members' assumptive worlds. Members come each Sunday presuming a basic continuity between what they already know and what they will read or hear.

Presumptive responses cause individuals to make some typical mistakes that limit learning. These mistakes include overconfidence, an availability bias, recency effects, and vividness effects.

When we are overconfident, we are sure we already know enough to make a decision. The result is a confirmation bias. We favor data that supports our present beliefs. We dismiss data that contradicts our current opinions. Overconfidence always results in premature foreclosure and a failure to learn.

An availability bias causes people to gather information that is readily available. The most readily available data, however, may not be the most relevant for the discussion. People reach for available data without asking what kind of information they need to make a wise choice. Church members are particularly prone to this mistake. It takes time and energy to get the facts needed to make a good decision. But many church members operate under pressure and make decisions based on the most readily available data rather than the most useful data.

Rather than gather data about the issue under discussion, people sometimes draw parallels between the current situation and a recent similar experience they faced. Rather than examine the present reality on its own merits, they presume that it is just like another recent experience. This is described as a recency effect.

Similarly, a vivid experience or fact is more easily remembered. It is thus more readily available to the memory and more easily used. Although this vivid experience may be only slightly relevant to the situation, it overpowers more appropriate data.

"We have a real financial crisis here," said Jack Gracie, Covenant Church's treasurer. "Income is way behind what it should be. We are at the end of May and the church should have received five-twelfths of our projected annual income. But we are more than $10,000 short."

"These numbers are really alarming," Betty Farmer exclaimed. "Based on what you are saying, I think we better start cutting our expense budget tonight."

"Absolutely," Mark Bryce added as other heads around the table began to nod.

"You are assuming that people pay their pledges in equal monthly amounts. But is that really how the money comes in?" asked Sarah Hernandez. "It would seem to me that some months would be high and others low. You can't just divide the year into twelve equal amounts. Do you have any month-by-month income figures for the past few years?"

"No, I don't. But I do have these numbers, and they show a problem," Jack answered. Other voices murmured approval.

"Well, these may be the numbers most available to us," Sarah continued, "but I think the most readily available numbers may not be telling the whole story. I would like a better picture of the month-by-month trends before we start making cuts."

"I know it will be a lot of work," Martin Fairchild said, "but Sarah is right. The numbers that are most available may be misleading us about what is really happening."

"I agree with Martin and Sarah," Reed Butler interjected. "I am remembering that presentation last winter. The one where the pastor talked about biases in our thinking that can lead to poor decision making. I think we may have an availability bias here. And that may not be the only bias at work. Some of us may actually want to cut the budget. There are people here who were unhappy with the budget we adopted last fall. They are looking for numbers to confirm we made a mistake."

"You're right," observed another board member. "I really appreciated the pastor's presentation. It has been helpful in a lot of areas of my life. I think this may also be a recency or vividness error. We had a real crisis last year. Because that was such a painful experience, some of us may be seeing red flags too quickly. I think Sarah is right. I would like more information and some discussion to disentangle all these biases before we start cutting anyone's budget."

Short-Circuiting
Presumptive Thinking

According to Daloz (1986), it takes an almost Herculean effort to encourage people comfortable with their existence to think critically rather than presumptively. Sometimes only tragedy or a major unanticipated crisis can shake us out of the narrow mental models and assumptive frameworks in which habitual thinking imprisons us. Yet, Daloz continues, people can help to break this pattern of presumption when they toss bits of disconfirming information into conversations or ask questions about what others currently believe. "Cow plops on the road to truth," he writes, "invite [people] to entertain alternatives, to close the dissonance, accommodate their structures, think afresh" (224).

A well-placed question can short-circuit presumptive thinking. Asking rather than telling creates room for learning. Church members sometimes expect their leaders to provide solutions. Church leaders often succumb to these expectations, becoming experts in giving answers. But the real leadership challenge is to ask the right questions. Leaders, Bennis and Nanus (1986) propose, are problem-finders rather than problem-solvers. Effective leaders pose good questions rather than provide quick solutions. The right question can reframe a situation, helping people identify new angles of vision and alternative solutions.

What makes a good question? Our education has prepared

us to tell others what we think. But who has taught us the art of asking good questions? According to Zimmerman (1995), good questions are dialogic. They are dependent on the conversation and not the person for their focus. "They draw their potency from the field of meaning, not from autobiographical thoughts," Zimmerman notes (109). Good questions not only seek to deepen meaning, they also establish focus for a meaning-making conversation.

Zimmerman identifies three different types of questions: rhetorical, categorical, and cross-categorical. Rhetorical questions usually do not expect an answer. They are, therefore, unproductive questions to ask. Yet they are often our most common type of question. *"Don't you think we should . . .?"* we ask. When we ask this type of question, we really do not expect an answer. And our audience automatically adopts a defensive posture. Categorical questions limit the range of responses to specific categories. A *what* question asks for a label. A *where* question asks for a place. A *why* question asks for a justification. These are good questions to ask if we want more information, but they are not particularly productive if we are trying to make meaning. Meaning-making questions are usually cross-categorical. A cross-categorical question "searches for meaning by generating new contexts or reframing the group focus" (111). They "amplify the meaning that has been created by the group, allowing it to ebb and flow in many directions" (111). These are questions that do not have answers already embedded in them. *"How did you come to that conclusion?" "What would authentic faith look like if we saw it in this congregation?"* Such questions sound simple enough, but they are difficult to ask properly.

Karen Upchurch sat in her study and reviewed the worship committee's meeting that had just ended. It had been a frustrating experience. No matter what she said, no one spoke. All she heard the whole evening were her own monologues. "What could I have done differently?" she wondered aloud. "No matter how I tried to ask a question, everyone just sat there, staring at their hands."

"Well," Martha Bays offered, "I think it is difficult for people to answer questions quickly. Most of us have to think before we speak. You usually do not give us enough time to gather our thoughts."

"What do you mean?" Karen responded.

"I counted how long you would wait for an answer. At most, you would hesitate about one second. Then you would jump in with your own answer. Even if we do have an opinion, we need more time than one second to gather our thoughts. After a couple of your questions, I began to wonder if you wanted us to answer. So I stopped trying to respond."

"You mean I should wait longer before I give my own answer?" Karen asked.

"That's right. An instructor in one of my teacher education workshops told us to count to ten after we ask a question. I'm usually pretty uncomfortable with silence. So when no one answers, my anxiety takes over and I give the answer myself. By counting to ten, I break the pattern and give people time to collect their thoughts."

"I guess I never thought about it that way," Karen said. "What else do you see me doing?"

"You tend to ask 'why' questions. When I hear a question that begins with 'why,' I feel like I am back in the seventh grade being interrogated by my parents."

"You mean that instead of saying, 'Why were you upset about the choir's anthem?' I could ask, 'What feelings did the choir's anthem prompt for you?'"

"That's right. Another thing you could do is ask a more specific question. If you ask something general, then I don't really know how to respond," Martha continued, "so I just give you a conventional answer, the one I think you want to hear."

"So instead of asking, 'What makes worship meaningful?' I could ask something like, 'As you think back over the past month, can you name something in worship that really spoke to you?'"

"Now you've got the idea!" Martha exclaimed.

Asking questions, creating settings where people feel safe enough to discuss unpopular ideas, sequencing new information so that people are not overwhelmed, and building a collaborative contract for learning are four ways church leaders can minimize nonlearning responses. But church leaders are also called to foster environments that maximize learning at the speed of change.

Nurturing Learning Responses

Being too busy is one of the major reasons for nonlearning. "Although learning is intimately bound up with action, a potential learning situation arises only when action cannot be performed unthinkingly" (Jarvis 1992, 85). This underscores another paradox of learning: The faster the speed of change, the more we need to slow down our thinking.

Learning needs to be slow because our minds work so fast. This makes us subject to endless leaps of abstraction. Our mental models allow us to jump too quickly from one observation to a broad generalization. We substitute our mental model for the actual facts. This model then guides how we think and act. Errors frequently develop in our thinking and acting because of this rapid, inaccurate reasoning.

We learn when we slow down and monitor how we are thinking and acting. Jarvis (1992) calls this a creative or experimental response to a potential learning situation. Learning happens when people step back from the world of action, reflect on what has gone before, decide what they want to do, and then monitor their actions as they unfold.

Church leaders maximize learning when they create free, open, and hospitable spaces in which the need to act is temporarily suspended and people can think about how they are thinking. Two strategies are particularly useful in recognizing and challenging leaps of abstraction. The first is a ladder of inference. The second is a belief-behavior chain.

A Ladder of Inference

Argyris and Schon (1978, 1992) propose that we move up a ladder of inference as we move farther away from direct observation. The higher we go, the more our thinking becomes subject to errors. Each rung represents another level of mental assumptions that we have acquired. Each takes us potentially farther away from directly observed facts (see figure 3). We usually make errors because we leap from the first rung to the higher ones, assuming that our inferences are accurate.

Creative learning occurs when we render explicit the mental categories that shape each rung's inferences. The higher rungs, in particular, help us to identify and critique the mental models into which we have been socialized by previous experi-

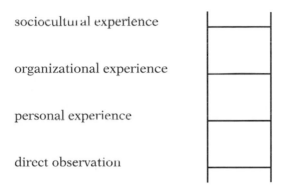

sociocultural experience

organizational experience

personal experience

direct observation

Figure 3. Ladder of mental assumptions

ences. As people surface their leaps of abstraction and analyze them in terms of a ladder of inference, learning is maximized. Greater understanding and more flexible thinking emerge.

Mary attends a meeting chaired by Jim. Jim comes without an agenda. He does a poor job of focusing the discussion. Nothing gets done. The next month Mary meets with the nominations committee. She says, "We cannot nominate Jim as a committee chair. He is unable to moderate a meeting."

"What did you see that makes you think Jim cannot chair a meeting?" asks Cyndy, another member of the nominations committee. "I have a very different perception of Jim, so I want to understand how you reached your conclusion."

"Well," Mary replies, "he did not have an agenda. He let a few people dominate the discussion."

"OK. That's your direct experience," Cyndy responds. She turns to the whiteboard and writes:

> Jim has no agenda, lets a few people dominate the meeting.

"Can you help me see how you get from that one particular meeting to a generalization about Jim's abilities. It feels like a pretty big leap, and I need to understand your thinking more clearly," Cyndy continues.

"Well," Mary says slowly, "if I really think about it, I had a pretty strong reaction to Jim during that meeting. His behavior seemed irresponsible. After all, everyone else was depending on him, and he let them down because he came unprepared. My parents were divorced when I was ten years old. Since I was the oldest child, I felt responsible for my brother and sister. I got them up in the morning, fixed breakfast, monitored their homework. I never had a childhood. I always had to be responsible. So whenever I see someone behaving irresponsibly, I feel angry because I never permitted myself to be that way even as a child."

"Let me see if I can get this on the board," Cyndy responds.

> I feel angry when I perceive someone as not acting responsibly.

> Jim has no agenda, lets a few people dominate the meeting.

"That helps me understand why you reacted so strongly to Jim. It also suggests that you may be projecting more onto Jim's behavior than just what happened in the meeting. Anything else?" Cyndy queries.

"In the previous congregation where I was pastor," Mary continues, "I watched a chairperson completely alienate a committee because she let a few strong-willed people dominate the discussion. In another congregation I worked with a governing board chairperson who never had an agenda and let the meetings run late into the evening. Eventually no one wanted to serve on the governing board because the whole congregation knew how poorly their time would be used. I vowed I would never let that happen again."

"That helps fill in the picture," Cyndy affirms. "It sounds like the experience in your previous church has become a model for how things work. And you just plugged Jim into that model based on what you saw in one meeting." Cyndy, drawing another rung on her ladder, writes:

> In my previous church an unprepared chairperson soured many people on volunteering for the governing board.

> I feel angry when I perceive someone as not acting responsibly.

> Jim has no agenda, lets a few people dominate the meeting.

"If I'm really honest, the whole culture puts a lot of emphasis on achievement, on getting things done," Mary observes. "In the church, we talk about grace. But I feel I'm judged on what I produce. If I don't perform, I'm out. So I thought that since Jim couldn't produce, he should be out."

"So there are some cultural and social assumptions at work here, too," Cyndy says, and then writes:

> I feel a strong need to succeed in this church.

> In my previous church an unprepared chairperson soured many people on volunteering for the governing board.

> I feel angry when I perceive someone as not acting responsibly.

> Jim has no agenda, lets a few people dominate the meeting.

"This is really helpful," Mary admits. "I am angry at Jim because I think he may sour people on volunteering for key committees and thus cause my ministry here to fail. But that's not very reasonable, is it?

"As I look at this, I may have leapt too quickly from my experience in that meeting to some generalizations about Jim. I cannot jump to the conclusion that Jim is going to drive people away from accepting committee assignments just because one meeting was not well planned. Maybe I should check out my perceptions. How have you experienced Jim?"

As Mary, Cyndy, and the committee continue their discussion, they discover that other members have seen Jim perform well as a committee chairperson. One member also shares that Jim's daughter was in a minor car accident the same day as the meeting. Although no one was hurt, the accident left Jim and his wife shaken. Dealing with the accident may have meant that

Jim did not have sufficient time to prepare for the meeting and was distracted.

When Mary later reviewed Cyndy's ladder of inferences, she realized the enormous leaps she made between her observation and her generalization. Building the ladder of inferences slowed down her thought processes and revealed errors caused by rapid processing of information.

Belief-Behavior Chain

A belief-behavior chain can also disentangle leaps of abstraction (Hawkins 1992). Figure 4 illustrates a belief-behavior chain. The items above the line are based in concrete, objective experience. The items below the line are usually hidden from view. Yet they profoundly influence how people feel and act toward the items above the line. My experiences do not directly shape my feelings. I put an interpretation on my experience that mediates between it and my feelings. This interpretation, shaped by my assumptions and mental models, may or may not be correct.

I am riding a bus. A woman in the next seat has several children traveling with her. They are shouting, fighting, and throwing things at one another. Occasionally one of these objects hits another passenger. The woman is completely indifferent to their behavior.

I interpret this woman's behavior as poor parenting. The longer this happens, the more angry I feel. Soon I am ready to say something sarcastic about her behavior.

Suddenly, the woman shakes herself out of a daze and says, "I'm sorry. My mother who lives with us just died. I'm going to the hospital to make arrangements and get her things. I just don't know what we are going to do."

My interpretation immediately changes. My feelings and my intended actions change just as quickly. When I do not examine the hidden assumptions behind my interpretation, I misread behavior and situations. How I categorize my experience can cause me to leap from an observation to the wrong generalization. Similarly, I leap from feelings to actions. I treat this as an automatic process, forgetting that hidden values influence how I will act on my feelings. Once I am aware that this world of hidden assumptions is at work, I cannot operate by presumption.

experience	feeling	behavior
interpretation	value-based decision	

Figure 4. How experience
and interpretation combine

DIALOGUE AND INQUIRY

Mastering the skills of continuous experiential learning goes hand-in-hand with developing a capacity for dialogue and inquiry. According to Watkins and Marsick, "When private meanings are made public, it is possible to examine the thinking that lies below the surface" (1993, 77). The ability to balance advocacy with inquiry allows us to examine our own thinking and to learn from our own experience.

Balancing Advocacy and Inquiry

Unfortunately, people sometimes employ a *mystery-mastery model* that works against dialogue and mutual inquiry (Argyris and Schon, 1978, 1992). Steps in this model are as follows:

1. Assume that someone else is causing your problems.

2. Develop a private diagnosis and solution for your problem.

3. Since the other person is responsible for the problem, get her to change. You can use one of three strategies to change the other person: (a) facts and logic, (b) manipulation and indirect influence, or (c) criticism in which you tell her what she is doing wrong.

4. If the other person resists, this confirms your original diagnosis that she is the problem.

5. Respond to resistance by intensifying your pressure or deciding you must protect her from "the truth."

6. If your further efforts are unsuccessful, it is not your fault. The other person is responsible.

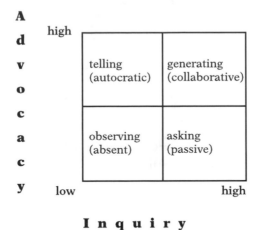

Figure 5. Advocacy-inquiry chart

Balancing advocacy with inquiry, Argyris and Schon (1978, 1992) contend, overcomes the tendency toward mystery-mastery thinking. When we engage in dialogue, we alternate between two basic behaviors. We either advocate our own opinions or we inquire into another's viewpoint. High advocacy means we only try to convince the other person that our views are right. Low advocacy means we do not. High inquiry is characterized by seeking to understand the other person's perspective. Low inquiry occurs when we make no effort to understand someone else's point of view.

Combining these options, people can fall into one of four positions as shown in figure 5. When a church leader combines high advocacy with low inquiry, she tells others what she thinks but does not ask what they think. Leaders who demonstrate low advocacy and high inquiry, on the other hand, never share their own opinions. They simply accommodate themselves to what others express. They are so busy trying to understand others that they never know what they are thinking or feeling.

This explains why both autocratic and passive pastors fail to promote learning. The autocratic pastor is so busy telling others what to do that she cannot engage in a true dialogue. She fails to help people surface hidden assumptions and challenge

What I Thought   What I Said

Self:

Other:

Figure 6. Mapping conversations and private thoughts

mental models. The passive pastor also fails to promote learn-ing. He is so busy listening to what others say that he cannot advocate his own position on an issue.

The real challenge is to combine high advocacy with high inquiry. When this happens, generative learning can occur. Everyone expresses openly what they think and feel while ac-tively seeking to understand the other person. Generative learn-ing is maximized when high advocacy is combined with high inquiry.

Revealing the
Left-Hand Column

Another tool that helps people combine high advocacy with high inquiry is also described by Argyris and Schon (1978, 1992). People map their conversations, using two columns as shown in figure 6. In the right-hand column, individuals record what was actually said and, in the left-hand column, they write what they were thinking but did not say. Once the whole con-versation is mapped, the speaker can review it for faulty rea-soning. The conversation need not be recorded verbatim. One's recollection, however imperfect, will identify faulty reasoning.

In examining the conversation, several questions help sur-face faulty reasoning, hidden assumptions, and inaccurate men-tal models:

1.   Did I tell others what I was really thinking?

2.   Did I try to convert the other person indirectly rather than say what I really wanted him to do?

3. Did I illustrate my thinking with clear examples so
   the other person understood exactly what I meant?
4. Did I try to get more information about how my conversation partner was thinking?
5. Did I question my own thinking?

Reflecting on these questions helps to clarify the balance between advocacy and inquiry. As one reflects on this material,
one may discover the faulty reasoning that typically blocks
learning and growth.

Pastor Damion Paige sat down a few minutes after Matthew
left the church office. What had gone wrong, he wondered. Yesterday was Matthew's first Sunday as the new junior high Sunday school teacher. From all reports, it had gone very badly.
Matthew then dropped into the church office this morning.
Damion felt that Matthew deliberately came by because he
wanted to talk about the class. Yet somehow it was a missed opportunity.

Deciding to learn more about how he thought and acted,
Damion took a piece of paper. On the right, he penciled the
heading: *What I Said*. On the left, he wrote: *What I Thought*. He
then filled in the chart (see figure 7).

As Damion reviewed the chart, he learned a great deal
about his own approach to difficult issues. He had not really inquired into Matthew's opinions or self-understanding. In fact,
he had been willing to let things remain pretty superficial. Furthermore, Damion mused, he had not shared honestly his own
thoughts. Everything he said was carefully guarded and vague.
The whole conversation had lacked either advocacy or inquiry.

By slowing down his thinking and looking at the thought
process behind his words and actions, Damion began to convert his raw experience into new meanings and new self-knowl-
edge that could shape his next conversation with Matthew.

SPIRITUAL DISCERNMENT,
CONVERSION, AND CONVERSATION

Untangling our leaps of abstraction involves discerning the
spirits that shape our thinking and acting. Cowan and Futrell
state that "the immediate object of spiritual discernment is inte-

What I Thought	What I Said
Everyone has told me that yesterday's class was a disaster.	*Damion:* How did class go on Sunday?
Does he not really know? Or is he not willing to bring it up with me?	*Matthew:* Well, you'd have to ask someone else. It was just our first class together. I think it will be OK.
This will buy me time. Maybe he'll say something that lets me figure out what he really thinks.	*Damion:* What do you think you will do next Sunday?
He must be scared to tell me. This comment just proves that he really lacks confidence in himself.	*Matthew:* I'm not sure. I'll look at the lesson for next week.
Probably whatever I say at this point is a waste of time. He's not ready to hear it.	*Damion:* Well, if you have any questions or need some help, just call me.

Figure 7. A map of Pastor Damion Paige's conversation

rior movements" (1988, 142). The goal of discernment is to discover the origin of these movements. "The means to identify the origin is to detect their orientation: are they moving one toward God or away from God?" (142). These interior movements are deeply intertwined with our hidden assumptions and leaps of abstraction. Discernment probes these depths to detect whether our assumptive worlds are orienting us toward or away from God.

One of the fundamental principles of discernment is to subject one's thinking to the judgment of others whom one trusts. As one engages in a prayerful conversation about the roots of one's spiritual movements, a new understanding of God's will can emerge. Dialogue, inquiry, and conversation are intertwined with discernment of God's will for one's life in a specific situation.

Dialogue, then, is not just something we do as we prepare for other, more important, tasks or ministries. Dialogue itself forms and transforms individuals within a people of God. Dialogue and mutual inquiry promote critical, liberating reflection on our assumptive frameworks. In this sense, there is a close relationship between conversation and conversion.

Some conversations can be shallow, empty, or even a means to hide from others and ourselves. On the other hand, if our conversations are occasions for mutual inquiry and dialogue, they hold open the possibility of conversion—a change of mind. While the exercising of leadership is usually associated with grander gestures, perhaps the key activity for leaders of learning congregations is to lead conversations. "Conversations give form to the reciprocal processes of leadership that make up the sum of the spaces or fields among us," writes Lambert. "Conversations are fractals of communities; that is, they recreate on a smaller scale the ecological processes of the larger community" (1995, 83). Conversation already points us beyond individual learning toward team learning, however. This is the topic of our next chapter.

6

Facilitating Team Learning

Teams are crucibles for learning. Through the give-and-take of dialogue, people cease being passive consumers of information. They create a collaborative community that actively constructs new knowledge. Group members learn in a continuous, almost random, fashion as they discuss common problems, exchange ideas, and work to achieve shared goals.

When individuals learn, they may or may not share their insights with others. But when a group learns together, members reinforce one another's learning. Teams help new ideas spread faster and further throughout a congregation (Watkins and Marsick 1993).

Just as there is no such thing as a solitary Christian, there is no such thing as a solitary learner. Most learning occurs when we interact with others. Meaning is a free flow, a stream, that moves in, among, and between people. When we think and learn, we are participating in a common pool of meaning that surrounds us like a great flowing sea. Our thoughts are not ours alone. Bruner (1966) and Vygotsky (1962, 1978) are persuaded that learning is always contextual and social. It is a cumulative experience derived from and informed by our social interactions with others.

Team learning has long been a central feature of Christian religious education. Most formal Christian education occurs in groups. The church school class gathers on Sunday morning. The Wednesday morning Bible study meets to discuss the coming Sunday's lectionary readings. Both settings encourage people to learn together by listening, speaking, and being in dialogue.

Formal Christian education is not the only place where team learning plays a prominent role, however. Boards, councils, and committees are crucibles for knowing-in-action. Church members seldom work alone in ministry. Their tasks are done with and through teams of people. These groupings are social locations where people are formed and transformed for ministry through experiences in ministry. They are occasions where people shape and reshape meaning in a community of shared practice.

Despite their importance, working and learning in groups can sometimes be a frustrating experience. Church meetings can be poorly planned, last too long, and never get to the important issues. A few outspoken individuals can dominate a class or a committee. Rambling discussions never get to the heart of a biblical text, a theological concept, or a ministry challenge.

Church leaders can equip themselves and others for better team learning through two key steps: (1) provide intentional orientation and training for ministry teams and (2) help church groups master the disciplines of team learning.

BUILDING LEADERSHIP TEAMS

Many congregations fail to train their lay leadership adequately. Individuals are recruited to serve on committees. But leaders neither orient these volunteers to their responsibilities nor train them for working and learning together. Although they are often hidden from view, high costs are attached to this failure to train new leaders. Ilsley (1991) found that duration of service in voluntary organizations was linked directly to the amount, kind, and quality of training that volunteers received. He also observes that volunteers who do not receive training are really learning that the organization's leaders place a low priority on the quality of their performance.

Mead laments that many congregations fail to provide training and orientation when new officers are elected and new board members begin their terms. "Every such change," he notes, "is an opportunity for new team building for the congregation's leadership. Most congregations are left to fend for themselves at these transitional times, with the result that few congregational boards operate very effectively" (1994, 81).

Leaders interested in cultivating team learning can ask themselves four questions: When should training occur? How should training be delivered? What level of training is needed? Where should training take place?

When Should Training Occur?

Leaders can offer training at two different points in a ministry team's development. They can train teams before they begin their work, or they can provide in-service training after teams begin their ministries.

Pre-Service Training

Pre-service training can include information about the congregation's history, organizational structure, goals, and values. New team members may also need basic information such as how to be reimbursed for expenses, how to get expenditures approved, how to reserve space in the building, insurance regulations, or other matters. Leaders planning pre-service training should not think any item is too simple or too obvious. The most obvious things may also be the very things a new team member is too embarrassed to ask about.

Later conflicts can be avoided if teams have such information before they begin their work. Some of this information, particularly policies and procedures, can be put in written manuals that the teams keep. This prevents information overload at a training event. It also gives team members a reference guide to which they can later refer. It is also important not to limit training to new board or committee members. The team as a whole is being trained, not the individual members. In addition, long-term members may need help learning about updated policies or changed procedures.

In-Service Training

In other cases, leaders may plan in-service training after a new ministry team begins its work. Sometimes team members do not know the right questions to ask until they have begun their work. Because they have not had an opportunity to do a particular task, they may not recognize the significance of information presented in pre-service training. In-service training allows teams to evaluate how they are working together and what skills or knowledge they need to improve their performance.

The choice between pre-service training and in-service training should not be considered an either-or decision. Planners of training events need to think through which option is best. They may also consider whether a sequenced combination of pre-service and in-service training is needed.

How Should Training Be Delivered?

There are three basic ways training can be delivered. Teams can (1) be given printed information to read or a video to watch, (2) participate in a workshop or seminar, or (3) be given a mentor or coach to work with them.

In general, the quality of learning is greatest when a mentor gives personal attention to team members over an extended period of time. Printed material, on the other hand, usually results in the least retention of new knowledge, skills, and values. In addition, the reader may misunderstand the material or overlook key information. Workshops or seminars provide an opportunity for team members to test out new skills or knowledge and to receive feedback in a supportive environment, thus helping them to internalize new patterns of behavior. Unlike having a mentor, these workshops and seminars are usually one-time events. Without ongoing reinforcement, new behaviors learned at such events can be forgotten.

Planners of training may find ways to sequence these three options. Sunday church school teachers, for example, might receive printed material outlining procedures and policies immediately after they are recruited. They then attend a workshop or laboratory school where they learn new teaching strategies and test these skills out in a safe, supportive environment. Finally, they are assigned a coach who works with them to plan class lessons or to advise them about discipline problems. This mentor may be a retired church school teacher or even a public school teacher who does not want to teach regularly in the church's Sunday school. The key to effective training is to think in terms of both/and rather than either/or. The crucial question is how to sequence different activities rather than whether to provide one or the other.

What Level of Training Is Needed?

Planners of training should consider three distinct levels of training: (1) *Level One*, orientation to the team's specific task; (2) *Level Two*, building the team's general skills for problem solving, decision making, or reflective thinking; or (3) *Level Three*, spiritual or personal enrichment.

Congregational leaders sometimes fail to provide even a basic orientation. When this happens, they inadvertently communicate that they are neither concerned for the quality of a team's performance nor care what a team accomplishes. Even worse, it may communicate that the nominations committee does not have any personal interest in the volunteer having a positive, successful experience. The opposite situation can also occur. Orientation is provided, but no one comes. Nominations committees sometimes communicate that orientation is voluntary—something the individual may or may not do. Consequently, new volunteers do not participate. What would happen if the nominations committee made it clear that participation in orientation and training was part of the position for which someone was being recruited?

Skill enhancement can cover a variety of topics: communication skills, handling conflict, problem solving, reflecting theologically. Some overview of group dynamics is also helpful. An introduction to group dynamics can help ministry teams weather the difficult times through which they must pass. Leaders who want ministry teams to engage in knowing-in-action will provide team members with tools and skills for thinking theologically and biblically about ministry.

According to Oswald and Matkin (1984), one of the leading causes of burnout among lay leaders is the lack of spiritual meaning in what they are asked to do. This highlights the importance of providing learning opportunities that enrich team members' spiritual and personal lives. It is not enough just to orient teams to specific tasks or to enhance their team building skills. They must be given resources to grow spiritually and personally through their ministries. This may mean a spiritual retreat or a time of Bible study and reflection built into particular meetings.

During the Lenten season, one congregation's committees set aside their regular agendas to participate in Bible study and prayer. In still another congregation, the nominations committee schedules a general orientation during January. They then schedule either skills enhancement workshops during the fall or a spiritual formation event during Lent. Bringing this intentionality to orientation and training requires an ongoing system for leader development. Too many congregations have a nominations committee whose work ends when they present a slate of officers to the annual congregational meeting. Congregations that have developed more intentional systems expand the nominations committee's work to include ongoing training and support for ministry teams. Other congregations, whose constitutions may limit the work of a nominations committee, have created special teams to oversee these efforts.

Where Should Training Take Place?

Planners need to consider where to offer training. Large and medium-sized congregations may have the resources to offer on-site training, using their own internal resources. Smaller congregations may not have these resources. But these congregations can work cooperatively with other churches in their community. In these cases, training is offered cooperatively at a local site beyond one's own congregation.

In many smaller communities, this approach has real advantages that extend beyond the congregation itself. Congregations may be the only source of leader development and training in these communities. The whole community's capacity is built when congregations work together with other local organizations to schedule leader training. Still other congregations may participate in seminars or workshops offered by conferences, presbyteries, districts, or regional church associations.

Leaders of learning congregations pay careful attention to how ministry teams are oriented and trained. They foster opportunities for teams to understand how their tasks fit into the congregation's larger vision, to enhance their skills, and to deepen members' spiritual lives. In addition, these leaders understand the disciplines of team learning and constantly monitor how committees, boards, and councils are learning together.

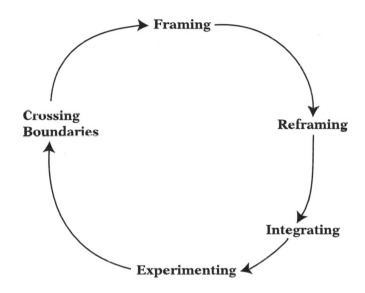

Figure 8, Five processes of team learning

MASTERING THE DISCIPLINES
OF TEAM LEARNING

Groups experience some predictable developmental stages as they develop their capacity to learn collaboratively and to work cooperatively. Unfortunately, groups can sometimes become stuck at one level and fail to make progress. Church leaders who understand these stages and phases are better equipped to diagnose a group's current developmental needs and to determine what is required for continued team learning.

The Five Processes
of Team Learning

How a team processes its raw experience will change over time. Understanding the different ways a group can process its experience will help church leaders evaluate its current capacity for learning. They are also better able to diagnose what the group may need to make progress. According to Watkins and Marsick (1993), these processes are framing, reframing, integrating, experimenting, and crossing boundaries (see figure 8).

Framing

My wife and I once purchased a watercolor depicting a seacoast village and some boats. Wanting to hang it on our living room wall, we went to an art shop to select a mat and frame. The salesperson placed various mats around our picture to see which we preferred. A blue mat drew out the vibrant blues of the sky and water. A brown mat highlighted the sand dunes with their pale green beach grass. The clouds fleeced up and skittered across the sky when an off-white mat was used. Once we had selected a mat, the whole process began again as we chose a frame. As we tried different frames, the watercolor's focal point and texture shifted. The frame or mat we placed around our picture determined what we saw within it.

This phenomenon is not limited to framing a picture. Our mental maps and assumptive frameworks filter what we see, feel, or experience. They draw attention to one aspect of a situation while blinding us to another.

Team members may discuss the same situation, but each person frames it differently. The conversation is diffuse and incoherent because many contradictory frames are being used. Participants are unaware how they and others are framing the situation. This lack of awareness limits learning and thinking.

Bolman and Deal (1991) identify at least four basic frames people use: human relations, structural, political, and symbolic. Those using a human relations frame tend to emphasize people and their needs. They look for ways to harmonize interests or to match individual needs with organizational needs. Structural frames, on the other hand, accentuate the importance of goals and purposes. Problems are attributed to poorly structured relationships between organizational tasks. The political frame highlights conflict, bargaining, and the use of power within groups. Symbolic frames focus attention on the meanings people attribute to events. They interpret events through the lens of ritual, myth, and story.

Two members of St. Paul's Church are locked in a bitter

conflict. The governing board's steering committee has decided to intervene. One committee member frames the conflict in terms of human relations, seeing it as a failure to communicate. If a mediator could just get the antagonists to talk honestly about their feelings, the situation would be resolved.

Another member wraps a structural frame around the conflict. He notices that one antagonist is the finance chairperson and the other is the chairperson of the board of trustees. Because the congregation gives these committees similar tasks, they have overlapping functions. This overlap ensures conflict. The solution is not to get the two antagonists talking. It is to restructure the church's committees so that the two chairpersons are no longer stepping on each other's turf.

Still other members put a political frame around the dispute. The chairpersons represent two different clans or coalitions in the congregation. These groups continually vie for power and control. Irreconcilable differences exist between them. Neither improving interpersonal communication nor restructuring the congregation's committees will resolve the conflict. This is an issue of power, negotiation, and bargaining.

As they discuss the church fight, committee members talk past one another. Few understand how others see the conflict. Most are unaware of the particular frame they put around it. The conversation is frustrating and unproductive. Little learning occurs.

Reframing

Reframing involves becoming aware that others are framing the situation quite differently than we are. We identify our own frame and become aware that other participants are using different frames. We then work together to transcend our own frames, looking at the situation from multiple perspectives.

I am an amateur photographer. I see a scene that I want to put in my scrapbook. I lift my camera, focus the shot, and press the button. I take one shot—perhaps a second—and no more. A professional photographer, on the other hand, takes many shots of the same scene. All are taken from slightly different angles of vision that frame the scene differently. The professional knows that the real art of photography lies in the framing. By comparing all her photographs, each framed slightly differently, the professional finds the perfect picture.

Reframing involves the same process. By shifting between multiple perspectives and evaluating the relationships between different viewpoints, team members identify their frames and learn to compare competing perspectives. Leaders can ask several questions that help teams to develop this capacity (Russo and Schoemaker 1989):

1. **What boundaries have we set in describing the issue?** The narrower the boundary, the more limited the options. People can define a situation so narrowly that many possible dynamics and choices are dismissed as out-of-bounds. The opposite problem can also occur. People describe a situation so broadly that they cannot get a handle on it.

Alan Smith and Nancy Underwood serve on the education committee. The committee is discussing discipline problems in the Sunday school. Alan always has trouble limiting a topic. He frames the discussion at the societal level. He talks about how children return to empty homes after school. If the committee wants to do something about Sunday school discipline problems, then members should start an after-school program for latchkey children. The committee, however, cannot make Alan's leap from Sunday morning discipline problems to working parents and latchkey children. Alan's frame is so broad that the committee cannot get a handle on the topic.

Nancy has the opposite problem. She wants to know what the superintendent is doing during the Sunday school hour. He should be monitoring halls and checking classrooms, she argues. Nancy's frame is so narrow that it limits seeing larger relationships between classrooms, teachers, parents, and the Sunday schedule. Not much can be learned when so little experience is used for reflection.

The real challenge is to find the proper boundaries—boundaries that are neither too broad nor too narrow for significant learning and thinking to emerge. Asking people to clarify how they bound a situation and to explain their rationale helps to foster creative reframing.

2. **What reference points do we use to define success or failure?** An artist creates a focal point around which everything else in her painting is organized. Similarly, people pick reference points to order and frame a situation. American

automakers, for example, used each other as their reference points during the 1970s and 1980s. But they did not use Japanese automakers, much to the Big Three's dismay as they began to lose market share.

Many congregations use other churches of their own denomination as reference points. They therefore miss what other nearby congregations in their own community are doing. Likewise, does a small church use another small congregation as its reference point? Or does it turn to a large, urban cathedral church? The choice dramatically influences how the congregation perceives its situation and possibilities.

As team members surface their tacit reference points, they are better able to describe what their differing reference points include or dismiss. This expands options and encourages more flexible and fluid learning.

3. **Are we fitting the frame to the problem or the problem to the frame?** People sometimes make a problem fit their frame rather than see which frame best illumines the situation. We occasionally have ready-made solutions and look for problems where we can apply them. Shifting between several frames breaks this pattern. Team members learn not only their own biases but how others frame the same situation. Often the best solution works in several frames. Less effective solutions look good in only one frame.

Russo and Schoemaker (1989) offer a parable to illustrate this point. A restaurant owner is frustrated because cooks and servers are bickering over orders. The owner consults a number of specialists for advice.

First, a sociologist frames the conflict as a structural problem of status and hierarchy. The higher-status cooks do not like taking orders from lower-status servers. He proposes that everyone undergo sensitivity training.

Second, an anthropologist tells the owner he has a problem of cultural norms and sex roles. The male cooks resist taking orders from female servers. She suggests the orders be given to a male clerk who will then hand them to the male cooks.

Third, a psychologist uses a human relations frame. He defines the problem as sibling rivalry in which everyone is competing for the owner's attention as surrogate parent. He proposes a weekly counseling session.

Finally, the owner consults an information theorist. She

frames the problem as cognitive overload. Cooks and servers are faced with too many orders too quickly. The resulting overload causes cognitive stress, which manifests itself as bickering and fighting. She proposes that the owner install a computerized system to handle the orders.

The owner is confused by these different options and shares his predicament with a junior cook, who suggests the installation of a simple rotating spindle. Servers place their orders on the spindle. Cooks take the orders off in sequence as they turn the spindle. The owner takes this solution back to the consultants. The sociologist approves, saying this would align status differences. The anthropologist believes a spindle will depersonalize the initiation of action and separate it from sex roles. The psychologist notes that it will reduce personal interaction and eliminate sibling rivalry. The information theorist states that the spindle will increase the system's external memory storage capacity.

Everyone is happy with the junior cook's solution but for different reasons. The moral of this story is clear—if a decision works in several frames, it is probably a good one. A single frame decision, on the other hand, seldom provides a satisfactory solution.

4.   **What does our frame illuminate? What does it overlook?** Every frame has strengths and weaknesses. We notice only what our frame illuminates. But what does it overlook? What does it prevent us from seeing?

Faith Church cooperates with two other congregations to provide emergency shelter for battered women. Faith Church's social concerns committee is upset that they are putting more money into the project than either St. Luke's Church or Elm Street Church. One committee member asks a simple question, "If we were at St. Luke's or Elm Street, how would they answer this charge? How would they say we are benefitting more than they are?"

This question helps Faith Church's committee discover perspectives that they had overlooked—how the bulk of publicity goes to Faith Church since the shelter is located in their neighborhood; how St. Luke's provides more people even though it does not provide much money; how Faith Church is able to secure matching funds from a nonprofit agency largely through the connections and relationships provided by Elm Street. The question enables committee members to recognize aspects of the situation that they had overlooked. They consequently develop a more nuanced and finely grained picture of the situation.

Integrating Perspectives

Ultimately, groups do more than link everyone's opinions together like beads on a string. They synthesize divergent perspectives. This is different from finding the least common denominator. At its best, it triggers the emergence of wholly new ways of understanding reality.

The more we look at situations from only one perspective, the more limited our options and the shallower our learning. People who have only one perspective "react with a small part of themselves to a small part of their world. They limit themselves by paying attention only to what is close up, by focusing on the moment, and by posturing in defense" (Steinke 1993, 93). As people develop the ability to take multiple perspectives, "they move beyond limiting conditions by seeing what might yet be, by allowing time for things to process, and by responding with self-control and poise. They have a greater capacity to modify and shape their environment," Steinke concludes (94). They have a wider range of responses, a larger view of reality, and a longer perspective on time. This makes their thinking much more flexible and complex. Because they think about people or events from multiple perspectives, they synthesize a wider range of possible options.

Some groups move too rapidly when integrating perspectives (Russo and Schoemaker, 1989). Other groups are little more than debating societies. They talk about various possibilities, but they never integrate these perspectives. The ideal process combines divergent thinking with convergent thinking.

The English word *dialogue* comes from Greek words meaning "through the word." New truth is discovered between us as we engage in a learning dialogue. *Discussion*, on the other hand, comes from the same root as *percussion* or *concussion*. It means "to bat around," "to hit." It is a more combative, competitive image.

Dialogue encourages divergent thinking, while discussion results in convergent thinking. "In dialogue different views are presented as a means toward discovering a new view. . . . In a discussion, decisions are made. . . . Discussions converge on a conclusion or a course of action. On the other hand, dialogues are diverging; they do not seek agreement, but a richer grasp of complex issues" (Senge 1990a, 247).

Church leaders facilitate team learning when they help groups to clarify whether they are engaged in dialogue or discussion. Vella (1994) describes this as the difference between a consultative voice and a deliberative voice. Learning is frustrated when some group members think they are exploring a topic while others believe they are making a decision. Leaders need to enable groups to sequence their explorations so that people have ample time for both dialogue and discussion. Furthermore, team members require clarity about which mode the group is using at a particular moment. Learning is limited when people are confused about whether the group is speaking with a consultative voice through dialogue or with a deliberative voice through discussion.

Experimenting and Crossing Boundaries

Experimenting and crossing boundaries are the final processes of team learning. A team experiments by trying a new behavior or an alternative strategy. It learns what will happen when it probes or explores a situation.

Alan Smith, Nancy Underwood, and the education committee have reached some consensus about Sunday morning discipline problems. They next experiment by asking two experienced public school teachers to provide mentoring for newer church school teachers. Most of the discipline problems have been reported among these newer teachers. The committee's experiment is designed to see whether this move makes a difference. Feedback from this action shapes their next response and leads to further experimentation.

The education committee also crosses boundaries. It discovers that children consume large amounts of sugary snacks during coffee hour just before Sunday school. So they discuss the discipline issue with the nurture and fellowship committee, which also experiments by providing alternative snacks. The education committee next approaches the nominations committee and asks it to include training in classroom discipline as part of the orientation workshop for new church leaders.

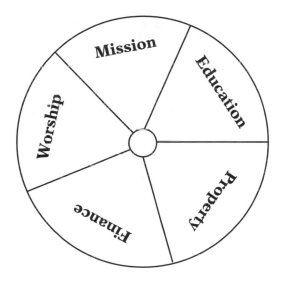

Figure 9. Rob's committee pinwheel

Implications for
Pastoral Practice

Pastors and educators can use their awareness of these learning processes to diagnose what a team needs to help it function more effectively. For example, if team members appear to be talking past each other, then the pastor or educator can help them move from framing to reframing. She can teach specific skills that help the team take on multiple perspectives.

Rob DeSilvio was frustrated with his governing board. Each member came to the board meetings representing one of the church's key committees. Members understood that they were there to defend their committee's particular interests and turf. Whenever something controversial came up, members kept repeating the same speeches over and over. No one listened to what anyone else was saying. They could not move past framing.

Exasperated with their performance, Rob decided to try an experiment. He took a large sheet of newsprint and drew a wide circle on it. Then he divided the circle into pie-shaped wedges.

On each wedge he wrote the name of a different committee represented on his governing board. He then put the paper circle on the floor and asked members to arrange their chairs around it, placing their seat directly in front of the wedge with their committee's name on it (see figure 9).

Rob then spun the circle. Suddenly the worship chairperson was seated directly in front of the wedge labeled "mission committee."

"I want you to tell me what you think the mission committee thinks about this issue," Rob instructed the chairperson. After she stated, as best she could, what the mission committee might think, Rob asked the next chairperson to take the perspective of the committee named on their wedge.

Once they had gone around the circle, Rob spun it again. This time everyone's chair was before yet another committee's wedge. Rob asked everyone to repeat the same exercise, taking the perspective of the committee wedge that had stopped in front of their chair.

They continued this process until everyone had experienced several rounds of perspective-taking. Then Rob asked them to discuss how it felt to take a different perspective. How did they speak differently? Did they listen with a different ear? Had they learned something about themselves? About the other chairpersons? About the issue?

This prompted a lively discussion and broke through the impasse that had prevented meaningful learning and work. Rob's exercise was a simple one, yet it moved the group from framing to reframing.

Similarly, if a ministry team seems stuck at the process of reframing and unable to move forward, then a leader might ask members to discuss the boundaries they are using, the reference points they are assuming. Likewise, a group that is stuck at the integrative process may need help sorting out whether people are speaking in a deliberative or consultative voice. Is this dialogue or discussion? Diverging or converging?

Four Phases of Team Learning

As a group of individuals becomes a learning team, they also move through four distinct phases. Each phase is characterized by a different learning style. These four phases are frag-

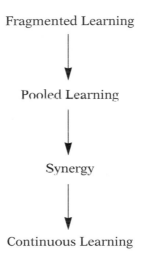

Fragmented Learning

Pooled Learning

Synergy

Continuous Learning

Figure 10. Four phases of team learning

mented learning, pooled learning, synergy, and continuous learning (Watkins and Marsick 1993). (See figure 10.)

Fragmented Learning

When a team initially comes together, individuals may learn, but they do not share or exchange their learnings with others. Participants keep new insights to themselves. Because participants' judgments may or may not be accurate and these perceptions are privately held, errors in thinking can persist. Individual framing is closely connected to this phase of team learning.

Linden Avenue Church recently began a Wednesday morning Bible study. The group rotates between participants' homes. After some coffee and light conversation, members discuss the coming Sunday's lectionary texts. During the first few weeks, discussion is superficial and limited to questions that seek basic information. Some group members acquire new information about the Bible and gain new knowledge. The whole group does not benefit, however, because individuals keep these personal insights to themselves. In addition, some group members reach inaccurate conclusions about the texts. Errors persist because each participant's learning is private and not subject to public scrutiny or correction.

Pooled Learning

Individuals now begin to share their perceptions with others. This sharing usually begins within a subgroup of the whole team. Only later does it spread to the whole group. Pooled learning is related to the reframing process. People move beyond their own personal frame and discover other perspectives.

In Linden Avenue's study group, three individuals carpool to the meetings. They share their insights and conclusions as they ride to and from the class. Soon they are shifting between these frames. These frames are set side-by-side, rather, and integrated or synthesized.

Synergy

As trust builds, the team jointly constructs shared meanings. Subgroupings give way to a fuller formation of the whole team into a learning community. A common language develops as a learning community forms. Ideas are tested and explored. New possibilities emerge that no one had previously considered. "In dialogue people become observers of their own thinking," writes Senge. "People in dialogue also begin to observe the collective nature of thought" (1990a, 242). The learning process of integrating perspectives can occur in this phase of team learning. Errors are still possible. They are less likely because people use the whole team to test their perceptions and judgments.

Linden Avenue's midweek study group now becomes more lively. Participants do not want to leave. The teacher comes with a lesson but is surprised when the conversation takes unexpected turns that delight and excite participants. No one can predict what will be said. The discussion flows naturally and creatively.

Continuous Learning

Team synergy becomes so contagious that team members use it everywhere. Group members export their new learnings throughout the congregation. "A learning team continually fosters other learning teams through inculcating the practices and skills of team learning more broadly" (Senge 1990a, 237). This phase is closely related to the team processes of experimentation and crossing boundaries.

Participants in Linden Avenue's study group introduce insights from their study group into other church committees. "When we discussed last Sunday's Gospel reading," one member says at a mission committee meeting, "we realized how all of us are missionaries right here. I think that's relevant to our committee's work tonight." Another study group member introduces some questions about how people frame issues into a board of trustees meeting. She shares tools and strategies for learning with which the trustees are unfamiliar.

Implications for
Pastoral Practice

Church leaders who understand the phases of group learning are better able to modulate their expectations for a group. For example, some pastors may expect synergy the first time a group meets. He or she might be wiser to expect that learning will be fragmented during the first few meetings. Trying to force the team to perform at a level several phases ahead of where it currently is functioning may frustrate the group so that members just silently sit through the meetings or may even quit coming to the meetings.

A pastor or church educator who understands these phases may also adjust her or his teaching style to fit the group's developmental phase. For example, during the phases of fragmented or pooled learning, it may be difficult for team members to engage in dialogue. Trying to force dialogue prematurely on the group may foreclose its learning. Instead, the leader might decide that the first few sessions are more appropriately times for lectures (if it is a study group) or for fact-finding (if it is a work team). As the trust level builds and synergy emerges, the leader can move to dialogue and discussion.

Forming

Storming

Norming

Performing

Figure 11. Four stages of group development

The Four Stages of Group Development

The five processes and four phases of team learning are intertwined with the four stages of group development. Here, however, attention focuses on how group dynamics contribute to team learning. Four easy terms have been coined to remember these stages: forming, storming, norming, and performing (see figure 11).

Forming

When groups are forming, people do not know one another. Trust is low. Participants may be uncertain about their role in the group, the group's goals, or what behaviors are acceptable. Their main decision is whether they will stay in the group or will drop out (Schutz 1975). The key question is, *Am I in or out?*

At this stage, the group is leader dependent. The leader must intentionally state the group's purpose and define the norms for how participants will treat one another or make decisions. Leaders are responsible for setting the group's emotional climate and modeling appropriate norms. Church leaders sometimes confuse being authoritative with being authoritarian. This is a time to be authoritative. At the end of this stage, the group has an agreed-upon purpose and clearly stated norms for its work. The key learning process at this point in the group's development is framing. In addition, participants are still experiencing fragmented learning.

Storming

Groups naturally evolve toward the next stage: dissonance. Privately held expectations about the group are gradually surfaced and discussed. Differences in perceptions and expectations create conflict. Relationships become stormy. This process occurs in two subphases.

First, members struggle over who has the power to shape the team's processes and decisions. Different subgroupings form. These coalitions test whether they have power to influence the team's decisions. The key question for this stage is whether or not I have power. Team members no longer ask, Am I in or out? Instead they ask, *Am I up or down?*

Group leaders are sometimes uncomfortable with this conflict. They want everyone to remain "nice." They become anxious when members are unhappy. If the leader suppresses this dissonance, participants cannot publicly negotiate common understandings of power, purpose, or norms.

The whole team must appreciate how dissonance is essential for their growth as a learning community. If successfully managed, this substage concludes with group members giving up unrealistic, private expectations. They instead negotiate more honest, realistic, shared goals and norms.

The second substage involves conflict with the leader. Once a group has coalesced around shared norms and goals, it tests its newly discovered strength by rejecting its designated leader. This leader can later be invited back as an equal partner rather than as an authority figure. Insecure leaders derail groups at this point by refusing to let groups reject them. They reassert their control at the very moment they should allow the group to take responsibility for its own life. Leaders need to remember that this is a natural phase in a team's development. It is not a personal attack on them or their leadership.

Church leaders can help groups to move through this stormy stage by equipping members with the disciplines of reframing. Understanding the dynamics of fragmented learning and pooled learning also enables church leaders to better facilitate group development during this stage.

Norming

Norming refers to the emergence of predictable patterns and routines in the group's life as it becomes productive in accomplishing its work. People play the same roles in every meeting. A strong group identity develops. People tell jokes or stories that only others in the group understand. Having spent time together, trust develops and people feel safe sharing ideas or feelings with one another. People at this stage ask, *How close or distant do I want to be to others in this group?* This particular developmental stage correlates to the synergy phase of group learning and the learning process of integration. Once again, leaders cannot focus solely on group dynamics. Attention must also be given to how the group is progressing through the sequential phases of group learning and whether they are mastering the processes of team learning.

Performing

At the performing stage, groups are able to focus on their task. They have developed routines for handling their work, they have agreed-upon norms and goals, they trust each other. Perspectives and possibilities are challenged, reframed, synthesized, and tested in action. The processes and structures that support team learning are now taken for granted and recede in importance. At this point, the team has moved to the learning processes of experimentation and crossing boundaries. The learning phase of continuous learning has also been reached. Leaders now carefully monitor not just the group's performance but also its learning processes.

Discipleship, Learning, and Community

Following Jesus is sometimes interpreted only as a matter of one's personal relationship with Christ, exclusive of relationships to others in a community of faith. As a pastor I visited families who hung pictures of Jesus on their walls. Jesus was usually alone in these paintings: Sallman's Head of Christ, a laughing Jesus, Jesus the Good Shepherd, the Sacred Heart of Jesus. These depictions profoundly shape our spiritual lives. They imply that we can have Jesus all to ourselves. They suggest that Jesus's ministry occurred without substantial involvement in a community of people.

The Gospels, however, usually describe Jesus amid a crowd of people, sitting at table fellowship with others, preaching and teaching the multitude, gathered with his disciples. Jesus is typically surrounded by those he loved and forgave, by those he invited into communion with himself and one another. Jesus gathered around himself a community of disciples. Discipleship happened in a community of learners.

We too discover life's deepest meanings as we live, learn, and work side-by-side and arm-in-arm with others. The disciplines of team learning are the means through which we grow in discipleship. These disciplines are more complex and difficult to master than those of individual learning. They draw us out of our solitary perspectives and invite us to adopt a more complex, fluid, and flexible stance toward reality. Despite their difficulty, they are essential for the creation of learning congregations.

Churches, more than any other organization, understand the corporate nature of thinking and learning. Jesus did not just instruct isolated individual learners. He created a learning community that could think, grow, and minister together. Jesus' call to discipleship is an invitation to participate in a learning community where people continually reframe their experiences and challenge their fundamental assumptive frameworks.

1

Cultivating
Congregational Learning

Human learning involves a relatively permanent change in the brain's biochemical make-up. New neural connections are forged, existing ones strengthened. These changes alter the mind's structure. Understanding how the human mind learns and changes is possible. But what does it mean for a whole congregation to learn?

Watkins and Marsick propose that systemic learning restructures an organization's long-term capacity for action in the same way that human learning changes our brain's biochemical make-up. They describe organizational learning as a changed "organizational capacity for doing something new" that is "embedded and shared through systems" (1993,147). This definition provides two guideposts for congregational learning.

First, learning congregations have formal, systemic ways to capture information and distribute it widely. They attend to feedback on their performance, environment, or history and convert it into meanings that guide congregational behavior. The flow of information in, through, and around a congregation is the primary source for its learning.

Second, by embedding new knowledge, skill, or values in their cultures, congregations preserve new learning and permanently expand their capacity for more complex behavior. Culture, Swidler proposes, is a "tool kit of symbols, stories, rituals, and worldviews, which people may use in varying configurations to solve different kinds of problems" (1986, 273). When congregations embed learning in their cultures, they make new knowledge, skills, or values available for future use.

Systemic or congregational learning complements the other two dimensions of our model—individual and team learning. Individual learning forms the foundation. Unless individual church members are equipped to learn and grow, little can be done to cultivate congregational learning or facilitate team learning. Team learning serves as a bridge between and catalyst for both individual and congregational learning. Teams are the link between individuals and wider systems. The final dimension—congregational or systemic learning—acts as a capstone for the learning congregation. It allows the congregation to embed newly generated knowledge, skills, and values into the community's ongoing life and to connect these new learnings to the larger environment in which it ministers.

CAPTURING AND
DISTRIBUTING INFORMATION

How congregations process information significantly determines their capacity for organizational learning. Congregations increase their learning capacity when they can capture information quickly, utilize it well, and distribute it effectively.

Dill has described an organization's environment "as a flow of information" (1971, 82). He proposes that "the continuing . . . influence of environmental inputs [is] the main source of learning and 'experience' within the organization" (86). He identifies five stages through which information is processed. How information moves through these five stages shapes congregational learning. Completing the chart in figure 12 may help church leaders better understand how their congregations capture and distribute information. Identify a recent action your congregation has taken. This may be either something entirely new or an adjustment in current programs or services. Who were the *triggers for action?* Who were the people or groups (formal or informal) that brought this situation to the congregation's attention? A formal group is an officially recognized board, committee, or council that is part of the congregation's ongoing organizational structure. An informal group is an unofficial network, caucus, or extended family unit. The education committee is a formal group. The retired men who

	Trigger for Action	Goal Information	Means to Goal	Constraints to Goal	Evaluate Performance
Individual					
Informal Group					
Formal Group					

Figure 12. Five stages of information processing

gather for coffee each Tuesday morning at the Country Charm Cafe are an informal group. Write the names of these triggers for action in the appropriate row of the first column.

In some congregations triggers for action are informal groups or isolated individuals. New members can also act as triggers for action. Established congregational leaders sometimes have a tendency to overlook these sources of information, however. Leaders are at the center of the congregation and talk to others in the center. Occupying formal roles and offices, they respond best to other formal groups and officers. They consequently have difficulty listening to voices on the margins. Learning congregations overcome this tendency by finding ways to listen to voices on the margins. They establish formal, ongoing processes that capture information from these sources and distribute it appropriately throughout the congregation.

In the appropriate row of the second column, write the names of the people, formal groups, or informal groups who provided *information about goals* in the identified situation. Who brought information about what the congregation could accomplish? It is important to note whether these names are individuals, formal groups, or informal groups.

In one congregation, a group of younger parents were triggers for action. They pointed out that the church provided very poor nursery care on Sunday morning and no childcare at other events. They insisted that poor childcare limited participation by younger families. This informal group did not provide information about possible goals, however. The age-level coordinator for adult ministries outlined specific actions the congregation could take. The shift from an informal group to a formal role legitimated the original information and shaped how it was transformed into congregational learning and action.

Some congregations distribute and tally surveys asking members for their opinions, perceptions, and goals. These surveys are intended to serve as triggers for action. But sometimes these results are not converted into specific goals either because leaders do not possess the skills to transform the raw information into compelling goals or because they are threatened by the directions suggested in the information.

In other congregations, individuals and groups have personal goals for themselves and the congregation but these goals are usually not made public. Individuals have personal visions for the congregation but leaders have not created public processes that surface these expectations and focus them into a common vision capable of motivating people.

In still other congregations, a few elite members or groups determine congregational goals. What these leaders describe as passivity and apathy might better be called a refusal to support congregational goals that do not reflect the passions, interests, or values of most members.

Examine carefully the pattern of names and groups in the transition from triggering action to identifying goals. This pattern strongly shapes the congregation's capacity to capture and distribute new information. Learning congregations capitalize on their triggers for action by having formal ways to convert information into meaningful goals and to share these goals throughout the congregation, mobilizing resources and energy.

In the third column, list the people, formal group, or informal group that provided information about the *means to achieve goals*. Many congregations have excellent goals and well-written mission statements. These documents remain filed away in a drawer, never to be acted upon. People know what they want to do. Yet they lack the skills to develop an action plan that moves them from where they are to where they want to be. They may not know what resources are needed to accomplish their goal. They may not know how to combine resources and action steps into a sequenced series of activities.

When a congregational system does not have the capacity to capture information about how to achieve goals, its learning capacity is diminished. Finding formal ways to gather and process this information is a critical component in fostering congregational learning.

In the fourth column, write the names of the individuals, formal groups, or informal groups that supplied information about *constraints to achieving goals.* "Many environmental inputs," states Dill, "serve directly or indirectly to constrain or to channel the direction in which the organization will move, not by specification of goals or of means to attain them, but instead by setting limits and restrictions on action" (1971, 84). Some of this information is very specific, such as the individual who points out that a raffle is prohibited by church doctrine. Other information may be more vague, such as rumors about how unnamed individuals or groups feel.

The more informally or individualistically a congregation processes information about constraints, the more it limits its capacity to learn. Congregations maximize learning when they create open, public processes through which congregational leaders can capture information about constraints, verify the accuracy of this information, and feed it forward into planning and action.

In the last column, list the individuals or groups that *evaluate organizational performance.* When this information is processed through individual or informal channels, there is little opportunity for the whole system to learn. The individuals involved may learn. The informal group discussing it around coffee and cake may discover new information. But this new knowledge, skill, or value does not spread very far or very fast throughout the whole congregation. Formal, public evaluation of activities is crucial to capturing and distributing what people and groups have learned through their ministries or in formal classroom experiences.

Groups not involved at earlier stages of planning and development are occasionally charged with evaluating a project. Yet they may understand neither the initial triggering event nor the goals that were developed. Congregational learning is maximized when the people or groups who initiated, planned, and implemented an activity are also involved in evaluating its results.

After completing the chart, leaders can analyze it for information-processing problems. When this exercise was used with a group of church leaders, some participants expressed shock as they realized their own name was the only one written across all five columns. Once the moment of initial dismay passed, participants explored how their own behavior limited congregational learning. They gained short-term satisfaction from "making things happen." Yet they failed to build congregational capacity for long-term learning. The exercise also helped them understand why they felt so overextended and burnt out.

Other participants discovered that some boxes were completely empty. This exercise gave one church leader new insight into why so many projects never got off the ground. People saw things that needed to be done, yet nothing ever happened. There were many triggers for action. But the congregation lacked formal processes to capture and distribute information about possible goals and the means to achieve these goals. This absence hindered the congregation's ability to learn, grow, and change. She returned home with ideas about how to create small task forces charged with goal setting and implementation that were more focused than her congregation's previous efforts.

Congregations enhance their capacity for learning at the speed of change when formal, ongoing ways exist to capture and to distribute knowledge, skills, and information. With this capacity, they are self-guiding, self-activating learning organizations.

A CULTURE THAT
PRESERVES LEARNING

Connecting the congregation to the larger environment and processing this new information is not the only strategy for cultivating congregational learning, however. Leaders of learning congregations also attend to how new knowledge, skills, and values are embedded in the congregation's collective memory so that they are available for future use.

The congregation's culture is critical for this process. Schein (1985) defines culture as the learned behavior of a stable community of people. Culture exists at three distinct levels. The first level includes what Schein calls "artifacts." These rest on the surface and are usually easily seen or experienced. They are daily activities, rituals, and events. Schein's second level rests just beneath these visible artifacts and undergirds their meaning. His second level encompasses statements about what people in the organization consider good or bad. These are usually offered to explain what is happening at the first level. Schein describes this as the values level of culture. Finally, organizational cultures are characterized by commonly held views of the world that have been formed over time. These basic assumptions, unconscious and implicit, are buried deep within the organization. They drive much of what happens at the other two levels.

Sims and Lorenzi (1992) describe Schein's basic assumptions using the term "cognitive consensuality." Everyone in an organization shares a common mental map of reality. They think about themselves and their world in similar ways. They process and evaluate information using the same mental models. As new members join, they are socialized into this common framework of basic assumptions.

Congregations, like other organizations, depend on these taken-for-granted mental models and assumptive frameworks for joint action. Shared understandings of how things are done form a basis for cooperation. A congregation's organizational life consists primarily of this shared mental map rather than the structural charts contained in books of discipline, order, or polity. This corporate, consensual mental map reflects the learnings that a congregation has preserved from its past experiences.

Elements of Culture

Elements of culture in which learning and meaning are embedded include (1) stories about the congregation's heroes and heroines, (2) symbols, and (3) rituals.

Stories

Stories about its heroes and heroines are an important window into a congregation's culture. According to Bolman and

Deal, "stories keep traditions alive and provide examples to guide everyday behavior" (1991, 296). Referring to the computer development team in Kidder's *Soul of a New Machine* (1981), Bolman and Deal observe that "stories about the dogged persistence and creativity of group members created an atmosphere that encouraged others to go beyond themselves" (297).

Heroes and heroines model how church members are expected to behave. Stories provide clues for what behaviors the congregation rewards and values. To rehearse a story is to preserve what was learned from an experience in an easily retrievable form (Ong 1982). As stories are told and retold, members rehearse preserved meanings that guide their actions.

Hope Church is a small, inner-city congregation in a changing neighborhood. Its members are older families who once lived in the neighborhood but now drive back from the suburbs. Neighborhood housing now serves economically and socially deprived families and older adults. After years of sealing itself off, Hope Church is attempting to minister to its immediate neighborhood. The congregation is creating new stories that preserve and rehearse what Hope Church's members have learned as they make this transition.

Bud Smith is the hero of one such story. Bud is a quiet, soft-spoken retiree. After the church was burglarized and a computer stolen from the church office, the police arrested a young man living near the church. The next Sunday, Bud's church school class complained about the burglary as another sign of their deteriorating neighborhood. Bud quietly asked if anyone had been to the county jail to visit the suspect. After an uncomfortable silence, Bud announced he would visit the prisoner.

This began a long-term relationship between Bud and a troubled neighborhood youth. As their relationship developed, Bud began to understand inner-city youth and their problems. He became more involved in neighborhood issues. He also shared his experiences with the Sunday school class and the church's governing board. Families living around the church soon noticed Bud's involvement and the church's changing attitude. His actions built new bridges of understanding between Hope Church and its community. Hope Church frequently retells Bud's story because it preserves and evokes what the congregation has learned about community outreach and neighborhood ministry.

Symbols

A congregation's symbols reflect embedded meanings and learnings. The Christian symbols of the Great Tradition—table, cup, font, or cross—may dominate a congregation's symbol system. More often, the most powerful symbols arise from the congregation's particular history and unique experience. Church leaders are so accustomed to the Great Tradition's symbols that they miss the importance of a local congregation's particular symbols.

Trinity Church's organ is one such local symbol. Several years ago, the organ was moved from the center of the chancel to a position along one wall. The communion table and cross were then moved to the center, becoming the focal point for worship. This shift occasioned bitter conflict and controversy. To manage the conflict, the governing board contracted with a church consultant. This consultant guided church members through a long process in which they thought theologically about worship, developed public processes to make a decision, and built consensus for a new worship design.

Trinity Church's organ now represents a powerful congregational symbol. It preserves what the congregation learned from its work with the consultant and makes these learnings available for future use. When faced with potential conflict, church members now invoke the organ as a symbol for how to deal with conflict and make decisions.

Etzioni (1968) describes symbols as "stored power." Congregational leaders do not need to resort to overt applications of power when they can use a symbol to mobilize people and resources. A symbol mobilizes people because it activates past meanings capable of guiding present action. Sims and Lorenzi (1992) similarly describe symbols as triggers that initiate preserved mental maps and action scripts. Trinity Church's organ represents stored power. This power can mobilize church members to consensus building activity and fair fighting behavior.

Rituals

Rituals are staged and predictable. They convey implicit meanings that may or may not be directly related to the activity itself. Their goal is to "explain, make things comprehensible, and provide meaning. . . . Rituals both mirror our ideas and shape them" (Bolman and Deal 1991, 265).

Congregational life is filled with rituals. When church leaders hear the word "ritual," they usually think of the formal rituals of the Great Tradition—worship, baptism, or the Lord's Supper. Church members engage in many other rituals, however. Some of these local rituals shape congregational behavior more powerfully than the formal rituals of the Great Tradition. Church leaders are sometimes so attuned to the Great Tradition that they underestimate the power of local rituals to form and transform a people of God.

St. Matthew's Church has an annual church bazaar. The explicit purpose is to raise money for church projects and world mission. These are not the only—or even the most important—purposes, however. Elaborate rituals surround this annual event and convey powerful implicit meanings. Members learn what behaviors are rewarded and what values are prized as they participate in St. Matthew's bazaar. The arrangement of the booths reflects power, importance, or status in the congregation. The food booth provides a ritual location for personal conversation and renewing friendships. The items crafted by different church organizations and displayed on the tables reflect congregational values and identity.

Church meetings are another source of ritual behavior. Some rituals occur as people arrive for committee meetings. Others happen in the hallway or parking lot afterward. The meeting itself may be a highly orchestrated ritual of minutes, correspondence, discussion, and voting.

Pilgrim Church, for example, went through a period of low self-esteem and membership loss. Blessed with an effective leadership team, the congregation looked at its corporate life, discerned a new mission, and implemented a revitalization strategy. Although these events happened more than a decade ago, members still engage in predictable rituals that preserve this era's learnings. Meetings follow a ritual pattern of personal sharing, agenda confirmation, actions by consensus, and post-meeting evaluations.

Meeting formats and planning processes rehearse the skills and values learned during the time Pilgrim Church was redeveloping. These activities make past learnings available to new members. They also keep the whole congregation from forgetting what was learned during its redevelopment.

Implications for Leading
a Learning Congregation

Pastors and other church leaders have always understood that they are responsible for conveying the content of Christian faith to individuals. They have paid less attention to how they equip a whole congregation to make meaning of Christian faith. Story, symbol, and ritual are important strategies for leaders who want to cultivate systemic learning.

Mobilizing Local Stories,
Symbols, and Rituals

Leaders engage in at least two cultural activities that enhance a congregation's capacity for learning. First, they cultivate the meanings either explicitly or implicitly present in the congregation's current culture. Second, they ensure that new stories are told and new symbols are preserved.

Church leaders wanting to understand a congregation's mental map listen carefully to its stories. They observe its symbols and note its rituals. These artifacts and beliefs express the congregation's basic assumptive framework. They reveal what the congregation has preserved out of its past experience. Leaders work to activate these past meanings and to direct their stored power to positive ends.

Church leaders also build learning capacity by creating and embedding new stories, symbols, and rituals in congregational life. This preserves newly acquired knowledge, skills, or values for future use. If a crisis moment passes and is forgotten, key learnings are lost. The congregation is doomed to repeat the same pattern again.

St. Mark's Church was in a growing suburban area, yet its membership was declining. Its building was poorly maintained and needed extensive repairs. The congregation's story conveyed the message that it was a small, impoverished church. Congregational stories communicated how poor the church had always been. The heroes and heroines were people who saved the church from financial calamity by digging into their own pockets. Congregational rituals and ceremonies did little to reinforce any sense of cohesion and identity. Committee meetings were rituals where members rehearsed the myths and stories of poverty and ineffectiveness.

Hector Cortes, a new pastor responsible for church redevelopment, was assigned to the congregation. As he listened to people and read through old records, he found alternative stories and symbols that preserved a more positive image of the congregation. These sources contained stored learnings for how the congregation had once coped with change and ministered effectively. Old newspaper clippings told of community outreach efforts fifty years ago. One article described the congregation's efforts to organize a community theater group. Another article, written when St. Mark's was the first public building in the community to install electric lights, spoke of the congregation as innovative and ready to try new things.

Hector took advantage of every opportunity to revive these forgotten stories and to rehearse them in church communications and personal conversations. He promoted these stories, substituting them for stories of poverty and helplessness. Congregational stories—like stories in general—have interpretive keys. A few critical events are selected out to structure the narrative carrying congregational identity. Other incidents and events are overlooked, however. The whole narrative is changed when different critical events are used to construct the narrative framework. This, in turn, alters the congregation's core identity and culture.

When past symbols and stories could not be found, Hector created new ones. Stories about present members engaged in creative ministry efforts were given prominence. These new heroes and heroines helped redefine the meaning of membership at St. Mark's Church. They communicated what behaviors were rewarded and valued, gradually reshaping members' expectations and performance.

St. Mark's governing board worked with the congregation to develop an ambitious redevelopment strategy. As part of this strategy, the board adopted a slogan for its new vision: "With God, All Things Are Possible." This vision statement was repeated endlessly on bulletin covers, letterhead, and newsletters. A button maker was purchased. Buttons with the words "With God, All Things Are Possible" were distributed to members. Members wore these buttons on Sundays and at church events.

Some members wore them to nonchurch events so they could tell others about their church. Gradually, these newer stories, role models, symbols, and rituals supplanted others that had immobilized and demoralized church members. The myth was gradually changed from being "We Are Small and Poor" to "With God, All Things Are Possible."

Over a number of years, the congregation redeveloped. While this success was due to a number of factors, Hector's ability to activate latent symbols and to create new stories was a crucial component.

Congregational Culture and Biblical Memory

Efforts to tap congregational culture cannot be limited to the resources of local history, ritual, or symbol, however. Birch notes that local stories are set within the larger story of God's continuing activity within the people of God. "A congregation's memory," he writes, "must reach back to find its roots in the biblical communities of faith or it will lose touch with those traditions that made the church Christian and not just one of many volunteer associations in society" (1988, 31).

Like a local congregation's stories, biblical stories preserve what earlier generations of God's people learned from their experiences. Too often a congregation's interpretive keys come from its own history and experience. Leaders of learning congregations help church members discern new, more adequate interpretive keys from Christian scripture and tradition. They equip congregations not just to learn from their own experience and history but from the larger Christian story.

"Memory plays a primary role in forming our identity, values, perceptions, dispositions, and intentions," Birch (1988, 30) observes. Without a long-term effort to implant biblical memory in congregations, references to the Bible "will only be sprinkled into the church's activities to lend justification to priorities already determined on other grounds" (30). He challenges church leaders to engage in the long-term, ongoing task of nurturing the images, insights, symbols, and stories of biblical faith in a congregation's life so that these resources are components of its cultural tool kit.

Birch (1988) makes several concrete proposals for how

church leaders can cultivate biblical memory. First, he says, laity must be empowered to nurture biblical memory. This means involving laity in tasks previously reserved for clergy: preaching, adult education, pastoral care. Second, religious education must recover the predominantly story-oriented character of biblical faith. Children need to learn biblical stories, not just morals drawn from scriptural passages or life applications based on biblical texts.

Third, membership preparation can be a vital means to embed biblical stories, symbols, and meanings in a congregation's culture. "Every group of new members to enter the congregation," Birch asserts, "provides an opportunity for renewal of faith memory by a group of those already members" (1988, 40). Over a period of years, such increased attention to study, reflection, and learning at a crucial transitional moment "can have a broad and profound effect on the availability of resources from the church's memory" (40).

A recovery of visual images and symbols in worship and church life also plays a critical role in cultivating congregational memory. The button at St. Mark's Church—"With God, All Things Are Possible"—represents one aspect of this process. A fifth possibility is increased attention to exegetical preaching. "Nothing could be more helpful in encouraging congregations to attend to the role of memory in their life than to hear preaching which is itself rooted in that memory in ways that demonstrate its power to address our lives and inform our mission," Birch (1988, 41) concludes.

The United Parish of Springfield illustrates how biblical stories and symbols represent stored power capable of mobilizing people for ministry. The United Parish's governing board engaged in a visioning process that began with a study of biblical images of the church. For six months, each monthly governing board meeting began with a 20-minute Bible study on a different image of the church. As board members grappled with these images and sought to name an image appropriate to their context, they were increasingly drawn to the dialogue in John 21.

Jesus' call to "feed my sheep" spoke to their own situation. People were going hungry in this urban community. They needed real food. The governing board invited the mission committee to explore opening a cooperative soup kitchen with some other congregations. But even those with full pantries need good, wholesome food. When the opportunity arose to host a local farmers' market on Saturday mornings, the governing board quickly responded. This activity, they concluded, was consistent with their vision of feeding God's people.

Soon the men's club began selling fresh doughnuts and coffee to shoppers browsing through the farmers' market. The money raised was given to the soup kitchen. This activity captured the multi-leveled meaning of feeding God's people. People were directly nourished with food and fellowship as they shopped for wholesome fruits, grains, and vegetables. The profits from this effort then went to feed the city's hungry and homeless.

Other groups in the church were also struggling with what it meant to feed God's people. Surely, people needed spiritual food as much as physical nourishment. How can our worship best feed people's deepest hungers, they asked. Since Christians are concretely fed in the sacrament of the Lord's Supper, the worship committee increased the number of communion services and worked to make them more meaningful. Coffee hour after worship was similarly reframed in terms of meeting people's physical and spiritual hungers.

The vision of feeding God's people became an organizing principle around which a variety of fellowship, worship, education, and outreach activities were structured. The stored power inherent in biblical stories and symbols overcame resistance to new ministries. The farmers' market was not just some committee's crazy way to create parking problems on Saturday. It reflected what Christ called this particular church to do. Changes in worship were not just some radical concept imposed by the pastor or the denomination. They were grounded in the congregation's own cultural identity as a place where God fed people both physically and spiritually.

LEARNING AS CAPACITY BUILDING

Congregational learning is capacity building. It enhances the congregation's competence to act in new ways. It increases the congregation's ability to gather, process, and distribute new knowledge, skills, or values generated through the practice of ministry. Church leaders cultivate congregational learning when they facilitate the free flow of information throughout the congregation. Open-ended communication encourages the fluid movement of ideas among all parts of the system. It creates a synergy for collaborative learning between the individual, team, and organizational levels of the congregation as it empowers church members for ministry at the speed of change.

As these learnings are embedded in symbol, story, and ritual, the congregation's capacity for future action is permanently strengthened. Leaders are charged with sheltering and shepherding the making of meaning in a community of shared practice. They cultivate a congregation's learning capacity by nurturing its long-term biblical memory and by monitoring how its symbols, rituals, and stories contribute to ministry among the people of God.

8

Congregations as the Context for Fundamental Change

We live during a time when there is more fundamental change than ever before. "We may be faced with a task that is also historically unprecedented, at the growing edge of our culture's evolution," Kegan suggests (1982, 218). The major challenge facing both individuals and organizations, he continues, is "how to fashion long-term relationships, even 'long-term communities'. . . which are the context for fundamental change rather than ended by it" (218).

Learning congregations are long-term communities seeking to be the context for fundamental change. Unless Christian congregations develop this capacity, they will surely be overwhelmed and ended by the speed of change. Our true greatness, Emerson (1965, 38) once observed, lies in our transitions. How people and institutions negotiate their transitions more clearly reveals their true character than how they maintain their permanence.

Serving as incubators for fundamental change, learning communities thrive on chaos (Peters 1988). They cultivate impermanence, encourage questioning, value experimentation (Redding and Catalanello 1994). These attitudes are not foreign to Christian faith. Indeed, they are at the core of what it means to be God's people. Although other institutions disappear, God's people survive across time and space precisely because they understand themselves as the context for fundamental change.

The Old Testament narratives of Abraham and Sarah reveal a people on the move, living in tents, flexible, creative, expectant.

Second Isaiah, heir to the same tradition and white-water rafting through his own turbulent historical transition, echoes Abraham and Sarah's openness and expectancy. Observing events around him, he hears God say, "I am about to do a new thing" (Isa. 43:19). Paul, looking back at these same narratives, describes them as modeling the very essence of a faithful response to God in Christ. "So, you see," he writes (Gal. 3:7), "those who believe are the descendents of Abraham [and Sarah]."

An openness to growing and changing is inextricably tied to our capacity to learn. Following Jesus entails an openness to growth, to going new places and accepting new tasks. "I tell you," Jesus told Peter (John 21:18, 19b), "when you were younger, you used to fasten your own belt and to go wherever you wished. But when you grow old, you will stretch out your hands, and someone else will fasten a belt around you and take you where you do not wish to go." After this Jesus said to Peter, "Follow me."

Following Jesus involves a commitment to learning. To be a disciple, as the very word suggests, is to be a learner. Jesus, speaking to his disciples on the night he was betrayed (John 16:12–13), told them "I still have many things to say to you, but you cannot bear them now. When the Spirit of truth comes, he will guide you into all the truth." The Holy Spirit gifts us with the capacity to learn, grow, and change. Guided by the Holy Spirit, who provides both the motivation and the direction for learning, congregations become long-term communities that are the context for fundamental change. They are places where people expect continuous learning, growing, changing, transformation.

Leaders of such communities foster continuous learning and support ongoing growth. Their members continually learn to do new things and constantly challenge the assumptions behind why and how they do what they do. They are equipped to think more complexly, to clarify the mental maps that guide their thinking and acting, and to discern ever more clearly the common ministry to which God calls them through Jesus Christ. These congregations have an open flow of communication that encourages the free movement of ideas and information. They are characterized by theologically informed members and by leaders who understand themselves as shaping meaning in a community of shared practice.

Buffeted by the speed of change, these communities hear

and respond to Jesus' call: "Come to me, all you that are weary and are carrying heavy burdens, and I will give you rest. Take my yoke upon you, and learn from me; for I am gentle and humble in heart, and you will find rest for your souls" (Matt. 11:28–29). This promised rest is not quiet inactivity or release from the challenge of growth, however. It is the rest that rafters know when their paddles move in rhythm with the swift currents carrying them through the rapids of change to a new heaven and a new earth.

Glossary

Assumptive frameworks—large, usually unconscious, mental frameworks into which our conceptual content (specific ideas, beliefs, or concepts) is fitted. They shape our perceptions, guide our attention, and direct our thinking and acting. These frames of reference are largely conditioned by the social, cultural, and familial systems in which we are embedded.

Availability bias—a tendency to make decisions or to evaluate situations based on the most available data, even though these data may not be appropriate for the situation.

Balancing advocacy and inquiry—the ability to balance the strong statement of one's own judgments or opinions with a strong inquiry into the assumptions behind someone else's judgments or opinions.

Belief/behavior chain—refers to the fact that our experiences do not directly shape our feelings or behaviors. An interpretation of our experience intervenes between the raw experience and our feelings.

Confirmation bias—a tendency to seek evidence that confirms what we already believe rather than to gather the facts, opinions, and judgments pertinent to the situation.

Culture—the learned behavior of a stable community of people. Culture exists at three distinct levels: (1) artifacts (daily activities, rituals, or events); (2) values (statements people make about what is good or bad); and (3) basic assumptions (commonly held assumptions about the world that are usually unconscious and implicit).

Framing—the process of seeing the same situation through a variety of perspectives. It involves understanding the assumptive frameworks behind one's own perspective as well as adopting temporarily the perspectives and assumptive frameworks of others.

Heroic leadership—an approach to leadership in which the leader is expected to have all the answers, to make all the decisions, and to take all the responsibility for everything that happens in her or his organization.

Ladder of inference—a technique for understanding the assumptions that underlie one's perception of a situation. The lowest rung on the ladder represents direct experience. The higher one goes on the ladder, the more levels of interpretation intervene between the actual experience and one's judgments about it.

Learning organization—a term used to describe a community of people where some or all of the following conditions exist: (1) individuals are always growing, learning, changing; (2) people are willing to examine both their own assumptions and those of others; (3) people express mutual respect for other people; (4) there is an openness to experimentation and a recognition that failure is sometimes the price of risk; and (5) the whole community is continually expanding its capacity to create its future.

Meaning-perspective—a term used by Mezirow (1991) to describe the large, usually unconscious, frameworks into which specific conceptual content is fitted. We are conditioned into these large frames of reference by our social, cultural, and familial experiences. *See also* Assumptive frameworks.

Meaning-schema—the specific beliefs, ideas, or concepts that are fitted into our meaning-perspectives. Whereas we are aware of the specific ideas, values, or beliefs we may hold, the underlying meaning-perspectives usually remain beyond our awareness.

Mental maps/models—*See* Assumptive frameworks; Meaning-perspective.

Mystery/mastery model—a way of dealing with other people in which we (1) assume that the problem is someone else's fault; (2) develop a private solution to the problem that is not shared with anyone else; (3) try to change the other person through logic, manipulation, or criticism; and (4) treat resistance as confirmation that the other person really is the problem.

Postfigurative culture—a culture where the future is expected to reproduce the past. Members of a postfigurative society assume that their way of life is unchanging, eternally the same. The older generation teaches these eternal truths to younger generations.

Prefigurative culture—a culture where the present is experienced as discontinuous with the past. The older generation learns from the younger generation.

Recency effects—a tendency to perceive a situation through the lens of another powerful experience that may have occurred recently. This recent experience may or may not be relevant to the present situation.

Revealing the left-hand column—a technique used to improve one's capacity for genuine dialogue with others. In the right-hand column one describes what was actually said. Then in the left-hand column one expresses what was thought but not said. The conversation can then be analyzed for how one's unspoken thoughts or judgments distorted the dialogue.

Bibliography

Achtemeier, Paul J. 1975. *The gospel of mark.* Philadelphia: Fortress Press.

Anselm of Canterbury. 1974. *Proslogion.* Edited and translated by Jasper Hopskins and Herbert Richardson. New York: Mellen Press.

Apps, Jerold W. 1988. *Higher education in a learning society: Meeting new demands for education and training.* San Francisco: Jossey-Bass.

Arendt, Hannah. 1958. *Human condition.* Chicago: University of Chicago Press.

Argyris, Chris, and Donald A. Schon. 1978. *Organizational learning: A theory of action perspective.* San Francisco: Jossey-Bass.

———. 1992. *Theory in practice: Increasing professional effectiveness.* San Francisco: Jossey-Bass.

Barry, William A. 1992. *Spiritual direction and the encounter with God: A theological inquiry.* Mahwah, N.J.: Paulist Press.

Barth, Karl. 1964. *God here and now.* Translated by Paul van Buren. New York: Harper & Row.

Bennis, Warren, and Bert Nanus. 1986. *Leaders: The strategies for taking charge.* New York: HarperCollins.

Birch, Bruce. 1988. Memory in congregational life. In *Congregations: Their power to form and transform,* edited by C. Ellis Nelson. Atlanta: John Knox Press.

Block, Peter. 1987. *The empowered manager: Positive political skills at work.* San Francisco: Jossey-Bass.

Boff, Leonardo. 1986. *Ecclesiogenesis: The base communities reinvent the church*. Translated by Robert R. Barr. New York: Orbis Books.

Bolman, Lee G., and Terrence E. Deal. 1991. *Reframing organizations: Artistry, choice, and leadership*. San Francisco: Jossey-Bass.

Bradford, David L., and Allan R. Cohen. 1987. *Managing for excellence: The guide to developing high performance in contemporary organizations*. New York: John Wiley & Sons.

Brookfield, Stephen D. 1986. *Understanding and facilitating adult learning: A comprehensive analysis of principles and effective practices*. San Francisco: Jossey-Bass.

————. 1987. *Developing critical thinkers: Challenging adults to explore alternative ways of thinking and acting*. San Francisco: Jossey-Bass.

Brueggemann, Walter. 1982. *The creative word: Canon as a model for biblical education*. Philadelphia: Fortress Press.

Bruner, Jerome S. 1962. *On knowing: Essays for the left hand*. New York: Atheneum Publishers.

————. 1966. *Toward a theory of instruction*. Cambridge, Mass.: Belknap Press.

Carroll, Jackson W. 1991. *As one with authority: Reflective leadership in ministry*. Louisville, Ky.: Westminster/John Knox Press.

Cervero, Ronald M. 1988. *Effective continuing education for professionals*. San Francisco: Jossey-Bass.

Cooke, Bernard. 1990. *The distancing of God: The ambiguity of symbol in history and theology*. Philadelphia: Fortress Press.

————. 1992. *God's beloved: Jesus' experience of the transcendent*. Valley Forge, Pa.: Trinity Press International.

Cooley, Charles H. 1991. *Human nature and the social order*. New Brunswick, N.J.: Transaction Publications.

Cowan, Marlan, and John C. Futrell. 1988. *The spiritual exercises of St. Ignatius of Loyola: A handbook for directors*. Hartford, Conn.: Jesuit Educational Center for Human Development.

Cremin, Lawrence. 1976. *Public education.* New York: Basic Books.

———. 1989. *Popular education and its discontents.* New York: HarperCollins.

Daloz, Laurent A. 1986. *Effective teaching and mentoring: Realizing the transformational power of adult learning experiences.* San Francisco: Jossey-Bass.

DeGruchy, John W. 1986. *Theology and ministry in context and crisis: A South African perspective.* Grand Rapids: Wm. B. Eerdmans Publishing Co.

Dewey, John. 1933. *How we think: A restatement of the relation of reflective thinking to the educative process.* Boston: D. C. Heath.

Dill, William. 1971. The impact of environment on organizational development. In *Readings in organization theory: Open-systems approaches,* edited by John G. Maurer. New York: Random House.

Durka, Gloria, and Joanmarie Smith. 1976. *Modeling God: Religious education for tomorrow.* New York: Paulist Press.

Emerson, Ralph Waldo. 1965. *Journals and miscellaneous notebooks of Ralph Waldo Emerson.* Vol. 5. Edited by M. M. Sealts, Jr. Cambridge, Mass.: Harvard University Press.

Etzioni, Amitai. 1968. *The active society.* New York: Free Press.

Evans, Sara M., and Harry C. Boyte. 1986. *Free spaces: The sources of democratic change in America.* New York: Harper & Row.

Fishburn, Janet. 1988. Leading: Paideia in a new key. In *Congregations: Their power to form and transform,* edited by C. Ellis Nelson. Louisville, Ky.: Westminster/John Knox Press.

Fossum, Mavis, and Merle Mason. 1986. *Facing shame: Families in recovery.* New York: W. W. Norton & Co.

Friedman, Edwin H. 1985. *Generation to generation: Family process in church and synagogue.* New York: Guilford Press.

Gellatly, Angus. 1986. *The skillful mind: An introduction of cognitive psychology.* Bristol, Pa.: Open University Press.

Giroux, Henry. 1988. *Schooling and the struggle for public life:*

Critical pedagogy in the modern age. Minneapolis: University of Minnesota Press.

Harris, Maria. 1989. *Fashion me a people: Curriculum in the church.* Louisville, Ky.: Westminster/John Knox Press.

Hawkins, Thomas R. 1992. *A life that becomes the gospel.* Nashville: Upper Room.

Heifetz, Ronald. 1994. *Leadership without easy answers.* Cambridge, Mass.: Belknap Press.

Holland, Joe, and Peter Henriot. 1983. *Social analysis: Linking faith and justice.* New York: Orbis Books.

Hull, John M. 1991. *What prevents Christian adults from learning?* Valley Forge, Pa.: Trinity Press International.

Ilsley, Paul J. 1991. *Enhancing the volunteer experience: New insights on strengthening volunteer participation, learning, and commitment.* San Francisco: Jossey-Bass.

Jarvis, Peter. 1992. *Paradoxes of learning: On becoming an individual in society.* San Francisco: Jossey-Bass.

Jones, Ezra E. 1993. *Quest for quality in the church: A new paradigm.* Nashville: Discipleship Resources.

Kanter, Rosabeth, Barry Stein, and Todd Jick. 1992. *The challenge of organizational change: How companies experience it and leaders guide it.* New York: Free Press.

Kegan, Robert. 1982. *The evolving self: Problems and processes in human development.* Cambridge, Mass.: Harvard University Press.

———. 1994. *In over our heads: The mental demands of modern life.* Cambridge, Mass.: Harvard University Press.

Kidder, Tracy. 1981. *The soul of a new machine.* Boston: Little Brown.

Kim, David. 1990. Total quality and system dynamics: Complementary approaches to organizational learning. Paper no. E40–294. Cambridge, Mass.: Sloan School of Management, Massachusetts Institute of Technology.

Knowles, Malcolm S. 1980. *The modern practice of adult education: From pedagogy to andragogy.* 2d ed. New York: Cambridge Books.

Krummel, Forrest. 1992. *A congregation's response to baptism in their educational ministry.* D. Min. thesis. Chicago: McCormick Theological Seminary.

Kung, Hans. 1968. *Truthfulness: The future of the church.* New York: Sheed & Ward.

Lambert, Linda. 1995. Leading the conversations. In *The constructivist leader,* edited by Linda Lambert et al. New York: Teachers College Press.

Langford, Thomas. 1991. Teaching in the Methodist Tradition. In *By what authority: A conversation on teaching among United Methodists,* edited by E. Price and C. Foster. Nashville: Abingdon Press.

Little, Sara. 1993. Rethinking adult education. In *Rethinking Christian education: Explorations in theory and practice,* edited by David S. Schuller. St. Louis: Chalice Press.

Lynn, Robert, and Elliot Wright. 1980. *The big little school: 200 years of the Sunday School.* Nashville: Abingdon Press.

Marchese, Theodore. 1993. TQM: A Time for Ideas. *Change* 25 (3):10–13.

Martinson, Roland D. 1988. *Effective youth ministry: A congregational approach.* Minneapolis: Augsburg Press.

Marty, Martin. 1993. Christian education in a pluralistic era. In *Rethinking Christian education: Explorations in theory and practice,* edited by David S. Schuller. St. Louis: Chalice Press.

Mead, George H. 1934. *Mind, self, and society: From the standpoint of a social behaviorist.* Chicago: University of Chicago Press.

Mead, Loren B. 1994. *Transforming congregations for the future.* Washington, D.C.: Alban Institute.

Mead, Margaret. 1978. *Culture and commitment: The new relationship between the generations in the 1970s.* Garden City, N.Y.: Anchor Books, Doubleday & Co.

Mezirow, Jack. 1983. Transformations in adult learning. Paper presented at the Annual Conference of the American Association for Adult and Continuing Education, Philadelphia.

———. 1991. *Transformative dimensions of adult learning.* San Franscisco: Jossey-Bass.

Mills, C. Wright. 1954. *Mass society and liberal education.* Chicago: Center for the Study of Liberal Education for Adults.

Moore, Mary E. 1983. *Education for continuity and change: A new model for Christian religious education.* Nashville: Abingdon Press.

———. 1993. Education in a congregational context. In *Rethinking Christian education: Explorations in theory and practice,* edited by David S. Schuller. St. Louis: Chalice Press.

Nelson, C. Ellis. 1971. *Where faith begins.* Richmond: John Knox Press.

———. 1989. *How faith matures.* Louisville, Ky.: Westminster/ John Knox Press.

Niebuhr, H. Richard. 1941. *The meaning of revelation.* New York: Macmillan.

Noll, Mark. 1994. *The scandal of the evangelical mind.* Grand Rapids: Wm. B. Eerdmans Publishing Co.

Ong, Walter J. 1982. *Orality and literacy: The technologizing of the world.* New York: Routledge, Chapman & Hall.

Osmer, Richard Robert. 1990. *A teachable spirit: Recovering the teaching office in the church.* Louisville, Ky.: Westminster/ John Knox Press.

———. 1993. Three "Futuribles" for the Mainline Church. In *Rethinking Christian Education: Explorations in theory and practice,* edited by David S. Schuller. St. Louis: Chalice Press.

Oswald, Roy, and Jacqueline Matkin. 1984. *Preventing lay leader burnout.* Washington, D.C.: Alban Institute.

Pai, Young. 1990. *Cultural foundations of education.* Columbus, Ohio: Merrill Publishing Co.

Palmer, Parker J. 1983. *To know as we are known: A spirituality of education.* San Francisco: HarperSanFrancisco.

Peters, Tom 1988. *Thriving on chaos: A handbook for a management revolution.* New York: Alfred A. Knopf.

Redding, John C., and Ralph F. Catalanello. 1994. *Strategic readiness: The making of a learning organization.* San Francisco: Jossey-Bass.

Rengsdorf, K. 1985. *Manthano.* In *Theological dictionary of the New Testament: Abridged in one volume,* edited by Gerhard Kittel and Gerhard Friedrich. Grand Rapids: Wm. B. Eerdmans Publishing Co.

Roehlkepartain, Eugene C. 1993. *The teaching church: Moving Christian education to center stage.* Nashville: Abingdon Press.

Rumelhart, David, and Donald Norman. 1978. Accretion, tuning, and restructuring: Three modes of learning. In *Semantic factors in cognition,* edited by John W. Cotton and Roberta L. Kalatzky. New York: Halsted Press.

Russo, J. Edward, and Paul J. Schoemaker. 1989. *Decision traps: Ten barriers to brilliant decision-making and how to overcome them.* New York: Simon & Schuster.

Schein, Edgar H. 1985. *Organizational culture and leadership: A dynamic view.* San Francisco: Jossey-Bass.

Schmidt, Warren H., and Jerome P. Finnigan. 1992. *The race without a finish line.* San Francisco: Jossey-Bass.

Schutz, William C. 1975. *Elements of encounter.* New York: Bantam Books.

Scroggs, Robin. 1977. *Paul for a new day.* Philadelphia: Fortress Press.

Search Institute. 1990. *Effective Christian education: A national study of Protestant congregations: A six-denomination report.* Minneapolis: Search Institute.

Senge, Peter M. 1990a. *The fifth discipline: The art and practice of the learning organization.* New York: Doubleday/Currency Books.

———. 1990b. The Leader's New Work: Building Learning Organizations. *Sloan Management Review* 32 (1): 7-23.

Sims, Henry P., and Peter Lorenzi. 1992. *The new leadership paradigm: Social learning and cognition in organizations.* Newbury Park, Calif.: Sage Publications.

Smith, John. 1968. *Experience and God.* New York: Oxford University Press.

Steindl-Rast, David. 1984. *Gratefulness: The heart of prayer: An approach to life in fullness.* New York: Paulist Press.

Steinke, Peter L. 1993. *How your church family works: Understanding congregations as emotional systems.* Washington, D.C.: Alban Institute.

Swidler, Ann. 1986. Culture in action: Symbols and strategies. *American Sociological Review* 51: 273–86.

Toffler, Alvin. 1991. *Powershift: Knowledge, wealth, and violence at the edge of the twenty-first century.* New York: Bantam Books.

Tough, Allen M. 1979. *The adult's learning projects: A fresh approach to theory and practice in adult learning.* Toronto: Ontario Institute for Studies in Education.

Vaill, Peter B. 1989. *Managing as a performing art: New ideas for a world of chaotic change.* San Francisco: Jossey-Bass.

Vella, Jane K. 1994. *Learning to listen, learning to teach: The power of dialogue in educating adults.* San Francisco: Jossey-Bass.

Vygotsky, Lev S. 1962. *Thought and language.* Cambridge, Mass.: MIT Press.

———. 1978. *Mind in society: The development of higher psychological processes,* edited by Michael Cole et al. Cambridge, Mass.: Harvard University Press.

Walker, Deborah, and Linda Lambert. 1995. Learning and Leading Theory: A Century in the Making. In *The Constructivist Leader,* edited by Linda Lambert et al. New York: Teachers College Press.

Walton, Richard E. 1969. *Interpersonal peacemaking: conflicts and third-party consultation.* Reading, Mass.: Addison-Wesley Publishing Co.

Warren, Michael 1994. Cultural coding and ecclesial re-coding in the young (part II). *The Gospel and Our Culture* 6 (3):2–3.

Watkins, Karen, and Victoria J. Marsick. 1993. *Sculpting the learning organization: Lessons in the art and science of systemic change.* San Francisco: Jossey-Bass.

Weick, Karl, and M. Bougon. 1986. Organizations as cognitive maps. In *The thinking organization,* edited by Henry P. Sims, Jr., D. Gioia et al. San Francisco: Jossey-Bass.

West, Charles, James Farmer, and Phillip Wolff. 1992. *Instruc-

tional design: Implications from cognitive science. Engle-wood Cliffs, N.J.: Prentice-Hall.

Williams, George. 1956. Ministry in the Ante-Nicene Church. In *The ministry in historical perspective*, edited by H. Richard Niebuhr and Daniel Day Williams. New York: Harper & Brothers.

Williamson, Clark, and Ronald J. Allen. 1991. *The teaching minister*. Louisville, Ky.: Westminster/John Knox Press.

Yoder, John Howard. 1992. *Body politics: Five practices of the Christian community before the watching world*. Nashville: Discipleship Resources.

Zimmerman, Diane. 1995. The linguistics of leadership. In *The constructivist leader*, edited by Linda Lambert et al. New York: Teachers College Press.

Index of Authors

Index of Subjects